emerge

A CALL TO LEADERSHIP

dr robert rush III

KP PUBLISHING COMPANY

ISBN: 978-1-950936-71-1 (Paperback)
ISBN: 978-1-950936-16-8 (eBook)
Library of Congress Control Number:

Editor: Frank Williams and Theresa A. Kirk
Cover Design: Juan Roberts
Interior Design: Jennifer Houle
Literary Director: Sandra L. James

Published by:

KP Publishing Company
Publisher of Fiction, Nonfiction & Children's Books
Valencia, CA 91355
www.kp-pub.com

Printed in the United States of America

Dedication

Much of my formative years centered around the connections and relationships that came together through one place, the church. I am a true church boy at heart. Our church was a powerful ministry that serves in Pacoima's community, a neighborhood in Los Angeles, California. In many traditional African American churches, the pastor is more than a preacher, but more like a community activist and leader. To be an effective pastor, one must understand the various nuances of leadership. I recall my childhood pastor, the late Apostle William T. Broadous, wearing many hats, of which I had the privilege of being a student, and I learned so much from him, I am grateful for how God used him and his focus on building the local church. His ministry was not fueled by the hopes of being famous but by his love for God and a sense of service to God's people.

It is my prayer that I can be that kind of selfless husband, father, son, brother, pastor, and leader.

This book is dedicated to the memory of Apostle William T. Broadous. May His legacy and faithful service live on through the countless lives he touched. I am grateful to him for training me and giving me the opportunity to grow as a leader. It is because of his leadership that I can do what I do today.

To my bride, Brittany P. Rush, you are a wonder! Thank you for always pushing me to be the best version of myself. Thank you for loving me unconditionally and being the woman of my dreams. It is my greatest joy sharing life with you. You have given me the best gifts humanly possible, our precious daughters. Thank you for allowing me to emerge!

To my babies, Gabrielle and Grace, you don't know it yet, but you both have been my greatest teachers. Thank you for bringing me so much joy and inspiring me to dream without bounds. I am confident that you two will grow up and change the world.

Contents

Foreword

When we look at the word leadership, it is understood that it carries weight. You have been given a responsibility to lead others, and you are now accountable for making a difference in the body of work you have been called to or that you are passionate about. We understand by historical documentation that everything rises and falls on the foundation of leadership. Without leadership, chaos and confusion can prevent, hinder, or delay anticipated productivity assigned to that body of work. No one is born a leader, but we all can become leaders through education and experience. Leadership is a decision to learn from others who can become mentors and coaches and impart to the student by education or example.

I want to introduce you to Dr. Robert Rush, who has the capacity to do both. He is a leader through education and experience. Dr. Rush is highly educated in this field of Emerging Leadership and has put together a comprehensive piece of work that will enlarge your capacity to lead in this present generation. This work is significant to those who want clarity and understanding of dynamics in leadership and how to apply the principles of leadership as they answer the call to lead.

I have known Dr. Robert Rush for many years, and he has become an example of leadership in the Christian community and the world at large. I encourage you to study this work, and by doing so, you will upgrade your ability to lead.

Dr. Rush documents the five stages he experienced as a growing leader; it is refreshing to follow his work in the five stages. He explains the seasons you will encounter as you journey towards maturation in leadership. I am excited about the documentation of the seasons or phases, starting with the invitation, then the apprenticeship; after that, the validation and confirmation that brings them to the fourth stage, the assignment season that produces the fifth and final stage called the legacy stage. This teaching will be instrumental in locating yourself in the leadership acumen and preparing you for the next learning steps that you will need to emerge.

I believe the work he has created will remove the cap of limitation from your life, no matter your age or occupation. These powerful principles are essential; they work across the lines of spiritual and secular endeavors.

His relevant and global approach in leadership is essential for anyone ready for next-level leadership. It is not just a good read, but it's thought-provoking and mind-altering in how he approaches leadership concepts.

This book is a bold challenge and call to action. So, if you are ready for expansion, keep reading and discover the blueprint of next-generation insights on leadership.

APOSTLE FRED L. HODGE, JR.
SENIOR PASTOR, LIVING PRAISE CHRISTIAN CHURCH
NORTH HOLLYWOOD AND PALMDALE, CALIFORNIA

Introduction

If you are reading this book, you probably have a longing or desire for more. You could be experiencing a sense that your life is intended for more meaning and purpose. I am excited that you are reading *EMERGE* and starting a journey towards influence and impact. Believe it or not, but every person has the potential to be a leader. It especially goes for believers. Every person who has accepted the Lord as their savior has the potential and assignment to walk into leadership.

In 2020, we experienced a rough year. The pandemic, the social unrest, the concern regarding the economy, and the political turmoil pointed to one main point: we are in desperate need of leadership. Our systems in America are seemingly failing due to the lack of solid and strong leadership. Companies are folding because people lack the acumen to lead and lead well. I will go as far as to say that we are in a leadership deficit as a nation and as a people.

I believe that this is the hour for people to rise up and take their seats! You are reading this book because you have been called to leadership.

In the year that King Uzziah died I saw the Lord sitting upon a throne, high and lifted up; and the train of his robe filled the temple. Above him stood the seraphim. Each had six wings: with two he covered his face, and with two he covered his feet, and with two he flew. And one called to another and said: "Holy, holy, holy is the Lord of hosts; the whole earth is full of his glory!" And the foundations of the thresholds shook at the voice of him who called, and the house was filled with smoke. And I said: "Woe is me! For I am lost; for I am a man of unclean lips, and I dwell in the midst of a people of unclean lips; for my eyes have seen the King, the Lord of hosts!" Then one of the seraphim flew to me, having in his hand a burning coal that he had taken with tongs from the altar. And he touched my mouth and said: "Behold, this has touched your lips; your guilt is taken away, and your sin atoned for." And I heard the voice of the Lord saying, "Whom shall I send, and who will go for us?" Then I said, "Here I am! Send me."

Isaiah 6:1-8

This passage opens talking about King Uzziah and the year he died. The Bible tells us that King Uzziah was a good king and did great things for the people he led. However, he got beside himself and made a prideful decision that caused him to get leprosy and eventually die. It was a devastating year for the people of Judah. You can imagine that it was a year of confusion for this nation, and they were in despair. In the Old Testament, we see a connection with prophets and kings. Sometimes prophets worked with kings and provided counsel for their reign, and other times prophets stood in opposition against the king, declaring words of judgment for their sin and poor leadership. Not much is said about Isaiah and Uzziah's relationship, but we can assume they were close. They were close enough for Isaiah to be with the nation at his sudden death and loss.

Judah and the prophet Isaiah are in mourning and are concerned about the future. The people are confused, but the Bible tells us that the prophet saw the Lord this year. Isn't it interesting that

WHEN THINGS SEEM TO BE THE WORST, WE CAN SEE THINGS CLEARLY!

when things seem to be the worst, we can see things clearly! In the year of confusion, the prophet was able to see the Lord on the throne. Isaiah's perspective was checked in the year of devastation. He set his perspectives into alignment. Sometimes God allows for everything to seem to be crazy so that we can get our perspective together. In the text, Uzziah, the natural king, had died, but the King of kings was still on the throne. I am not sure where you are in your life or what you have experienced personally, but I want to encourage you that the King of kings is still on the throne, and nothing can move him.

God allowed the prophet Isaiah to see things clearly and gave him a glimpse of the court of Heaven. He heard the Lord speaking of the need in the earth, saying, *"Whom shall I send, and who will go for us."* Isaiah 6:8

Let's unpack this! The king is dead, the people are in an up-roar, and the Lord sees the need. We see this same example in Exodus 3. In Exodus, the Bible tells us that the people of Israel cried out to God because of their oppression. The Bible also tells us that the Lord responded to their need by sending Moses to deliver His people. God's response to the crisis and the cry of the people of Israel in Moses' day was to raise and send Moses to be the people's deliverer. We see it in this scripture, God was aware of the state of the nation by expressing the need for one to be sent. Being sent depicts a person on a mission or a specific assignment. God needs to send one to the nation to give them His Word and to help heal their distress of losing their king. Isaiah was made aware of this activity, and he responded to the Lord, "Here am, I send me." The word "send" is the Hebrew word, *Hineni*. It is a word that speaks utter surrendering. This word gives the picture of a child responding to a parent in total submission.

> **BEING SENT DEPICTS A PERSON ON A MISSION OR A SPECIFIC ASSIGNMENT.**

In Genesis 22:1, we see the word, Hineni. The Bible says,

"After these things God tested Abraham and said to him, 'Abraham!'" And he said, "Here I am."

Abraham's response to going was, "Here am I." He said, "Here am I," before he knew what the outcome would be. Abraham was so connected and in love with God that he was willing to do whatever He asked. Essentially Abraham says yes to God before he knew the request. Little did he know that God would request for him to sacrifice his son Isaac. This was a crazy request because:

1. Abraham had struggled for years to have a child with his wife, Sarah.
2. Isaac was the son of promise, and the prophecy was that through Isaac, God would use Abraham's descendants to bless the entire earth. God has spoken to Abraham a word that seems impossible.

Through all the obstacles presented Abraham showed faith to believe God. Here we see serious testing of faith. The father of faith is now challenged to sacrifice what God had promised him. We know that this was a test. God was building a newer level of faith in Abraham.

When they came to the place of which God had told him, Abraham built the altar there and laid the wood in order and bound Isaac, his son, and laid him on the altar, on top of the wood. Then Abraham reached out his hand and took the knife to slaughter his son. 11 But the angel of the Lord called to him from heaven and said, Abraham, Abraham!" And he said, "Here I am." He said, "Do not lay your hand on the boy or do anything to him, for now, I know that you fear God, seeing you have not withheld your son, your only son, from me."

Genesis 22:9-12 NIV

I want you to get the full picture here. Abraham responded to God saying, "Here am I," and he went through the process of following through on completing God's request. It is here that we see *Hineni* a second time. As Abraham was lifting to slaughter his son, the Lord cried out to Abraham, and Abraham responded, "HERE AM I." Could you imagine the level of agony that Abraham must have had as he saw his promised son laying on the altar to be a sacrifice? Could you imagine the fear that Isaac had? Could you imagine the intensity of the moment as Abraham raised a knife to do something that he did not want to, but he was going to do because he had said yes to God? It was in the pinnacle of all this anxiety, fear mixed with emotion, that God calls, and Abraham still responsed, Here am I. God being the faithful God He is then instructs Abraham to not to sacrifice his son. It is also in the passage where we see God provided a lamb to be slain, and we get the word Jehovah Jireh from. Abraham said this in response to God's provision of the lamb.

Abraham's total yes to God caused him to be tested, but he received a greater revelation of God's love and provision. As you say yes to the Father and respond to the call you have been assigned, you will receive rewards that will blow your mind. Your provision is in your "Yes."

We also see this same word, *Hineni*, in Exodus 3:4 when God introduced Himself to Moses. Exodus 3:4

> *When the Lord saw that he turned aside to see, God called to him*
> *out of the bush, "Moses, Moses!" And he said, "Here I am."*
>
> Exodus 3:4

AS YOU SAY YES TO THE FATHER AND RESPOND TO THE CALL THAT YOU HAVE BEEN ASSIGNED, YOU WILL RECEIVE REWARDS THAT WILL BLOW YOUR MIND.

In this scripture, Moses is a fugitive prince who is serving in the wilderness as a shepherd. God revealed Himself to him in the burning bush. Moses did not know the God of his forefathers, but when God called, he responded, "Here am I." God was getting ready to raise Moses up as a prophet, a deliver, and a leader. Moses' position in life as a shepherd was a humble job. I am sure he would not think that he would be used to deliver a nation and perform many miracles. God's words to us are never predicated based on where we are now. God's words are always calling you from your current to your future. The prophetic word of God has the power to change your very existence. The response to God when He calls must always be, "Here am I."

Isaiah did not know what it would require of him, but he still responded to the Lord with, "Here I am, I am totally available."

This kind of response comes from a place of revelation. Once we understand God and His power, we should be willing to say yes to Him because His ways are beyond our ways and His thoughts are so expansive.

Isaiah had to see things clearly and be purified to be able to respond and be used by God to see the need for his nation and generation. God took Isaiah from

ONCE WE UNDERSTAND GOD AND HIS POWER, WE SHOULD BE WILLING TO SAY YES TO HIM.

a place of distress to a place of purification, to a place of assignment. Isaiah's response to God was powerful, and it changed the course of his life. Isaiah was in a position to receive his life assignment. The chaos of today's society speaks to the idea that we need people to rise up to the occasion and accept the calling to leadership. YOU ARE CALLED TO LEAD! There is a place in the earth that you have been called to rise up and reveal the heart of God. This is the hour where God is calling for His people to EMERGE!

YOU ARE CALLED TO LEAD!

CHAPTER 1

Leadership Defined

Imagine this; you see the job of your dreams working as a top executive at a large fortune 500 company. You heard about this job through an online resource, and you read the job description thinking that the job sounds like something you can do. You love the pay and can see yourself in the role. But, here is the kicker, you are completely unfit and unqualified for the position. I mean, completely incapable! You lack the emotional intelligence to deal with the demands of the subordinates, cannot lead at this level, never managed a team before, and are not equipped to manage the departments. However, you have the required education and can fudge with years' experience in this field. You are frustrated with your current job situation because you do not get along with your teammates and think you can lead better than your supervisor. You have a bit of a temper, and you don't receive constructive criticism well. You have been written up for insubordination, and you are not in the best standing with your bosses. You want out of your job, and the job you see online looks great. You say to yourself, "I should at least go for the role; the worst thing that can happen is they say no." You make sure your resume is stellar, your cover letter is impeccable, and you apply. To your surprise and excitement, the recruiter likes your resume and calls you in to interview for the job.

You know that you are a great presenter and communicator, so you feel you will have no problem breezing through the interview. You see, interviewing is easy for you because you are and have always been charismatic. You know how to be likable, and you used your abilities to connect with the hiring manager. You go through the interview process and feel confident because you have connected with the interviewers. Your conversation is about your family, your history, and your hobbies. You find out that you have a lot in common. You even have the same kind of dog. During the interview, you felt that you made a real connection. The problem is that your relationship is not based on talent, skill, intelligence, or ability; you are connected because they like you personally. You leave the interview feeling that you killed it, and you are confident that you got the job. You wait about a week to finally get that call. Yes, that call! The hiring manager calls you and tells you that you got the job. You are excited, and you celebrate knowing that you just got the position of your dreams. You know what they say, "Fake it until you make it."

The problem is that the departments and teams you will be leading are in a disastrous state. You see, what they did not tell you in the interview process is that past leaders destroyed the department because of their lack of competency. The teams are at war because of years of toxic work culture. The drama with the team is a byproduct of unhealthy management. They also didn't tell you that this job was extremely demanding, and they are depending on the person hired to save this part of the company from implosion. So you start the exciting new job that you did not receive because of talent, education, or skill, to find out that you are way in over your head. The team is too cantankerous for your charisma. The demand for the work exceeds your connecting ability. The organization is too chaotic. This team, these departments need a leader. You, unfortunately, are unfit because you have not been trained or processed for any role like this.

The world has a desperate need of leaders to emerge. Yet, it seems that in every sphere of influence, we see deficits relating to leadership. Organizations lack vision. People are unable to communicate. Businesses lack direction. We are in a state of emergency as it relates to leadership. At the height of the Covid-19 pandemic, I witnessed a desperate need for strong, decisive, integral leadership. No one had a clue as to what to do, and it took strong leadership to navigate those uncertain times.

I prayed earnestly about the nation's current state, and our lack of leadership and the Holy Spirit revealed to me that much of the lack I was seeing was due to vacancies of people who knew Him in seats of leadership. I was burdened with the need to inform, empower, and exhort people to step into their assignment of leadership.

> **THE WORLD HAS A DESPERATE NEED FOR LEADERS TO EMERGE.**

Leadership is defined as the state of position of being a leader—the person who leads and commands a group. In the world, we see different leadership models; depending on your education or privilege, you are invited to different levels of leadership. For example, a person with an MBA would have more opportunities to manage a team than a person with a high school diploma. As I previously mentioned, the world is in a desperate need of leaders to emerge.

> *And He said to them, "Go into all the world and proclaim the gospel to the whole creation.*
>
> Mark 16:15 ESV

This scripture is known as the great commission. It is in this commission that we find out about leadership. Jesus is speaking to His disciples and commands them to go into all the world and preach or proclaim the gospel of the Kingdom. To understand this in its entirety, we would have to understand the terminology of the disciple. A disciple is a dedicated follower of Jesus Christ, the one who accepts the teachings of Jesus as true. A disciple is a student of an instructor or teacher. Jesus is speaking to His students, informing them of the call in the earth. This commission is to go into all the world and share the message of Jesus. This assignment was not limited to a sector of believers or a special disciple. It is a commission to all who accepted the way of the cross.

We have heard this great commission for years, and we have been taught it, but it is apparent that there still are limitations as to how we carry this out. This commission is made to every believer. When we accept the truth of who Christ is, we are called to go into the world and impact it. This call is essentially a calling to be a leader and an influencer. It was a charge to each believer to go and develop ways to reach the world.

The calling to the disciples to reach the world could be easily interpreted as reaching the planet. It can also be interpreted as

> **WHEN WE ACCEPT THE TRUTH OF WHO CHRIST IS, WE ARE CALLED TO GO INTO THE WORLD AND IMPACT IT.**

reaching people groups and nations (although our assignment is to make sure all have heard the gospel of Jesus Christ). This calling is to reach every aspect of the world that impacts the lives of people. There are various worlds in the world. These are also looked upon as seven mountains or commonly known as different spheres of influence. I believe this commission calls for all disciples to impact the world by impacting people and everything that impacts people's lives and well-being. Knowing a "world" or "sphere" that you are called to impact is the foundation for understanding your assignment and leadership call. Your assignment is always connected to the world that you have been called to preach the gospel of the Kingdom to. Our mission is clear, to share and reveal the love of God to all men on the earth. This commission helps to give believers an understanding of our

> **OUR MISSION IS CLEAR, TO SHARE AND REVEAL THE LOVE OF GOD TO ALL MEN ON THE EARTH.**

assignment and calling. Assignment speaks of a task or work assigned to someone as a part of a job or course of study. A calling speaks of a strong urge toward a particular way of life. A calling gives you the idea of a mission, call, summons, or vocation. Everyone, especially every believer, has a particular calling. Callings are not only for preachers. We have all been called to carry out the great commission to the earth. Our assignment is the vehicle that we can use in carrying out that mission.

> **WE HAVE ALL BEEN CALLED TO CARRY OUT THE GREAT COMMISSION TO THE EARTH.**

LEADERSHIP IN SCRIPTURE:

Many people in scripture walked in leadership after they received their assignment or call. In many cases, the assignment was a call to leadership. We see this with Moses. All we know of Moses before his epic burning bush experience is that he is the adopted Hebrew son of Pharaoh's daughter, a fugitive, a shepherd and that his birth mother protected him because he was a beautiful child. For all that we know, he did not have a clue on how to lead a nation. We definitely know that he was not equipped to be a spiritual leader to the people of Israel. The grace for leadership came upon him after his encounter with the Lord and received the instructions. This call sent him on a journey that forever changed his life. Isn't it amazing how God never speaks to where you are, but He speaks to your potential? Moses did not know what he was made of until he was introduced to his destiny by a word from God. God's plan for His children's life is to prosper us in such a way that our influence is increased. Answering the call is a response to accept a role to influence. You have been called to be an influencer.

In the book of Judges, we see people rise up in leadership based on the need of the time and day. Many of the leaders that we see in those passages are not traditional leaders. These judges are responders. They say yes to God's call to action, and then the Lord makes them leaders.

David was not raised to be a king. David was raised to be a shepherd. When he was called and then anointed for his assignment, he received the anointing to lead. The anointing on his life made him qualified and skilled to be the second king of Israel. Do not allow yourself to be limited in accepting the call of God for your life. Your calling to leadership and greatness is not predicated on your history and past struggles. Your calling to leadership is all connected to the task that God has laid out before you.

Jeremiah 1:5 says, *"Before I formed you in the womb I knew you, and before you were born I consecrated you; I appointed you a prophet to the nations."*

The word "form" in this scripture, speaks of a potter and how they mold something into shape. The word also speaks of

7

treasure and something valuable. This verse can be looked at by God saying that He placed in us a special treasure before we were formed in our mother's womb. God knew us, placed the treasure connected with our assignment, and appointed us to accomplish something incredible. The treasure that is placed in everyone is connected with our life assignments. Appointed speaks for a predesigned purpose or plan. It is the destiny that you have already been called to do before you arrived here on the earth.

> Ephesians 2:10 says, *For we are his workmanship, created in Christ Jesus for good works, which God prepared beforehand, that we should walk in them.*

We were created in Christ Jesus to do good works. These works are our assignments in the earth. Every blood bought believer has been saved by Jesus to grow in faith and minister to the world. There is no salvation without assignment. Jesus has commissioned all his disciples to go into all the world and continue to make disciples of Christ. Living a life of leadership requires us to accept and do the good work that Christ has laid out for us to do. The development of leadership is to foster and discover these good works and to discover the treasure inside. Your life is bigger than just yourselves. Your life is bigger than just talent or ability. Warren Bennis says, *Becoming a leader is synonymous with becoming yourself. It's that simple and that difficult. Leaders are people who express themselves fully."*

Gideon - The least in My Clan -

Now the angel of the Lord came and sat under the terebinth at Ophrah, which belonged to Joash the Abiezrite, while his son Gideon was beating out wheat in the winepress to hide it from the Midianites. And the angel of the Lord appeared to him and said to him, "The Lord is with you, O mighty man of valor." And Gideon said to him, "Please, my lord, if the Lord is with us, why then has all this happened to us? And where are all his wonderful deeds that our fathers recounted to us, saying, 'Did not the Lord bring us up from Egypt?' But now the Lord has forsaken us and given us into the hand of Midian." And the Lord1 turned to him and said, "Go in this might of yours and save Israel from the hand of Midian; do not I send you?" And he said to him, "Please, Lord, how can I save Israel? Behold, my clan is the weakest in Manasseh, and I am the least in my father's house." And the Lord said to him, "But I will be with you, and you shall strike the Midianites as one man."

Judges 6:11-16 ESV

The Lord appears to Gideon while he is in the beating out wheat in the winepress hides from his enemies. When God spoke to Gideon, He did not speak to him as a scared, insecure young man. When God spoke to Gideon, He called based on his treasure. God spoke to him based on his potential. Gideon thought of himself as the weakest and the least, but the Lord saw him as a leader and deliver of a nation. God never speaks to you based on where you have been or where you are, God always speaks to you based on your future. God spoke to Gideon and was calling him beyond his bondage and insecurity. God spoke to Gideon calling him higher. Then the Lord says something amazing in verse 14 he says, "Go in this might of yours"—Gideon's might, and leadership ability, was his treasure. The issue was that he initially denied the truth of who he was supposed to become because his history said otherwise. Many times we hinder ourselves from moving in destiny because our personal history says that we aren't able to accept the call. Do not allow your history to hinder you! God desires for your history to be a testimony for your destiny. The Lord allowed you to have the story that you have, to make His call and anointing more significant. Your call to leadership is not based on your perceived ability or qualifications, your calling is based on your treasure.

> **YOUR CALL TO LEADERSHIP IS NOT BASED ON YOUR PERCEIVED ABILITY OR QUALIFICATIONS, YOUR CALLING IS BASED ON YOUR TREASURE.**

DISCOVERING YOUR TREASURE

But we have this treasure in jars of clay, to show that the surpassing power belongs to God and not to us

2 Corinthians 4:7

The Bible declares that we have "this treasure." This treasure is the message of the gospel of Jesus Christ. The gospel is the treasure of the saints. Being able to know the Lord and have His power through the cross is a treasure. It is through this treasure that we receive the Holy Spirit. The Holy Spirit's role in the life of a believer is to activate the power of the supernatural. The Holy Spirit does not only fill people to cause them to shake and fall out. The Holy Spirit fills people with power, and this power is the power to accomplish our assignment. We each have been called to preach this message. How we preach looks different, but the mandate is consistent. We have a world to reach. The treasure of the gospel requires an assignment. We must share this treasure to the world.

> **THE TREASURE OF THE GOSPEL REQUIRES AN ASSIGNMENT. WE MUST SHARE THIS TREASURE TO THE WORLD.**

Luke 12:48 tells us, *"To much is given, much is required."* God has invested a lot in you and with that investment comes great responsibility. All the talents, gifts, and abilities you have are for promoting the gospel of Christ. We must never forget the fact that we are in charge of glorifying God.

It is important to make sure that we invest in our self-discovery to discover our leadership assignment. Our purpose has nothing to do with us and has all to do with the Lord. Many people are confused as it relates to discovering our purpose. Many people cannot seem to get a handle on their why. I believe that the more we encounter Christ, the more we will be able to find our purpose. As we look into Jesus, we can see ourselves truly. Many people base their careers and life work on whatever story was sold to them. Some people use "passions" to influence their career paths. If we base our discovery on temporal things, then we will have temporal results. We can only truly find ourselves through the lens of Christ. He knows why we were created and how we can live the most fulfilled life. We see this with Apostle Paul before his conversion. As Saul, he persecuted the church, chasing after his passions. It was through his zeal that he was a part of the violent attacks against the early church. However, when he encountered the Lord Jesus, his vision for his life changed. He came to discover who he was born to be. He wasn't created to persecute the church, but he was created to propel the church. It is my prayer that as you read this book that you profoundly encounter Christ and that you will know why you were placed on the earth. It is my prayer that the eyes of your understanding be enlightened so that you may know the hope of calling.

> **WE CAN ONLY TRULY FIND OURSELVES THROUGH THE LENS OF CHRIST.**

We must consider what we want to do and, more importantly, seek to understand the why. Many people chase after dreams, and it is a result of the desires of the flesh. People pursue dreams for a lot of different reasons. Many people are drawn to success because of greed, the hopes of fame, the vision of grandeur, or even the influence to please or impress someone else. Our purpose should come from our encounters with God.

We cannot trust our intellect. I know you are smart and have a brilliant mind, but it is not dependable. Please hear me; I am not saying that you are crazy, but I am saying that you cannot trust yourself. We are fallen creatures, and we need to always bring our minds under the wisdom of the Lord in all we do. When Adam was created in Genesis, he was created to live in direct connection with the Lord. Adam and the Creator of the Universe walked together daily. Adam had the amazing opportunity to learn from the Creator about His creation. Until the fall of man, Adam and Eve both lived and received direct insight through the things that God spoke to them directly. In Genesis 3, we see how it all went down. Adam and Eve disobeyed God by listening to the serpent. When they disobeyed, the Bible tells us that their eyes were opened, and they knew that they were naked. Their disobedience opened their eyes to a life of darkness and wickedness. They then saw things differently than how they had seen before.

I used to work on Skid Row in Downtown Los Angeles. Skid Row is known to have lots of rats. I hate rats. So I made sure I left work in haste of seeing a rat. I am glad to say that I never saw a rat for three years. If no one had told me that rats were a problem in the area, I would never have known about the issue. My eyes hadn't been opened to that problem. Going back to Adam and Eve, evil was present in the garden, and their bodies could be used for sin, but they weren't aware of it. When they ate the fruit, their eyes were opened to their potential for evil. The story tells us that God was coming to meet them to spend time together and Adam and Eve were terrified. They knew that something was wrong and that they were not worthy to stand in front of a holy God. God says to Adam, "Adam, where are you?" Adam responded that he was hiding from God because he was naked and ashamed. Adam and his wife were embarrassed by their nakedness and decided to use leaves to cover themselves. Think about this, Adam has sinned, embarrassed because he is naked, and then thinks plants will give him the right covering. Adam represents us in our natural minds.

Yes, the leaves met a need, but it was not sufficient. In our mind, we make decisions for our life that may meet our needs, but it doesn't suit us well. For example, plants are not suitable to properly clothe human beings. The only way to have a clear understanding of what would work the best is to seek insight from our Creator. God would take animal skins and clothe Adam and Eve himself by the end of this story. Adam could not even dress himself in his mind; he needed the mind of God to help him. We must allow our vision for our life to be inspired by our times spent with the Lord. The more we encounter Him, the more we can understand His intentions and plans for our lives. Right now, I would like for you to pause and think if you are living your life based on God's plan for you or your plan for yourself. Have you been living life by God's design? I believe one of the primary steps to walking in an assignment is to accept God's vision for your life. We grow in the understanding of the vision through our time with God.

CHAPTER 2

Discovery— Who You Are?

I have a younger cousin named Ezekiel; I affectionately call him "Zekie-Beke." He is the son of my older cousin Lawrence, who has been an inspiration since I was a child. He is a USC grad and played for their football team. Lawrence is a beacon of hope for our family, and I have been blessed to have him as an example of excellence, tenacity, and strength. His wife Julie is also a USC grad, and she is a force of nature. Together they have built a successful business and raised some pretty incredible kids.

Ezekiel has always been an interesting kid. I mean, everything about him has been different. Now please hear me; I am not speaking of his difference negatively. In my opinion, he has been different in all the ways that you want a kid to be different. He has always seemed to have a pretty strong sense of who he is and has exemplified such strength as a young child. One day their family decided to go to an escape room for entertainment. For those of you who do not know what an escape room is, it is an

15

immersive, 60-minute, real-life adventure game. You and a team are placed in a themed room and have one hour to complete a mission and "escape" the room. Some missions can be escaping a prison cell or something like that. Other rooms are more mission-oriented, where a group has to find lost gold, launch a spacecraft, or compete with an art heist. Their decision to go was at the last minute, so they could not book the room they desired and had to book the most challenging room because it was all that was left. To know this family, you have to understand that each one of them is brilliant. Lawrence married a brilliant wife, and they have three brilliant children. So accepting this challenge was a fun adventure for them. They got into the room and found that it was indeed challenging. As a collective group, they struggled with the clues, and they were racing the clock to crack the codes needed to "escape."

The group got frustrated, but Ezekiel seemed energized by the challenge. He stepped up and began to lead the group and intently focused on cracking the codes and finding the clues to "escape" the room. Here is the thing, Ezekiel is known for struggling with staying focused when something doesn't interest him. He is the one that traditionally has a hard time staying on task. Due to his track record, he could have easily been expected to check out and get bored of this game. However, his response was the opposite of what was known of him.

My cousins Lawrence and Julie were amazed at his focus and analytical capability. He possessed the ability to think strategically and lead the group through frustrating challenges. He and his older brother took the ranks of leadership in the group and led the team in cracking the code. They won the challenge and escaped. This story is interesting because of Ezekiel's abilities that came to the surface for a need. He had never shown this strategic thinking before. His parents were astounded at how well he did. They were surprised because this situation brought something extraordinary out of him. They discovered a hidden treasure. I also believe that Ezekiel found something extraordinary about himself that day. It is amazing how sometimes we can only see our giftedness in times of pressure. It is interesting what is inside of us, and we have no clue it is there. I imagine that you are like Ezekiel; you are brilliant, full of skills that you don't know exist because you have not been put into a situation that pulls it out of you. You may even have done some amazing things, but you are unaware of your fullest potential. I believe we all have a treasure, and we must seek to find it and cultivate it.

Before we can discuss you and your calling to leadership, we must first do some soul searching to discover who you are. To locate your treasure and authenticity, you must first consider what you have been through. God has an amazing way of using all of our negative experiences for His glory. I have seen God take the worst stories and make them into amazing testimonies. When you look at what you have been through and consider what you have conquered, you can see how God desires to use the bad for His good.

Another main thing we must do as we discover who we are is to reflect and assess our passions. Your passions can let you know what will drive you. Money and "security" should never be a passion. Our devotional life allows our spiritual eyes to be opened so we can find our purpose.

> **YOUR PASSIONS CAN LET YOU KNOW WHAT WILL DRIVE YOU.**

In many cases, people end up working to make money and living an unfulfilled life. I have seen people work a job that they hate for 30 years, planning to retire to do their passion. I have seen these same people retire and never follow their dream because they don't have the vitality to accomplish them. Dedication is an indicator for purpose and provides a safe guideline in proper self-discovery.

In addition to assessing our zeal, we must consider our talents. Our talents and passions reveal to us the gifts that God has given us to accomplish our assignment. When we see our unique giftedness and allow it to be fostered through training, practice, and mentorship, we can truly walk in our destiny.

Gifts and talents are special abilities given to people to help accomplish our purpose on earth. Gifts should be discovered and developed. The reason why people are not able to make a living on passion is that their gifts have not been properly refined and cultivated. God is the giver of gifts, but we must make sure that we are great stewards of what He has given us. Excellent stewardship is the cultivation and the mastering of skills and abilities.

"Before I formed you in the womb I knew you, and before you were born I consecrated you; I appointed you a prophet to the nations."

Jeremiah 1:5

This verse reveals to us the nature of God regarding our purpose and assignment. We see that before the Lord created the prophet Jeremiah, He consecrated him to be a prophet to the nations. Before we came into this world, the Lord knew us and appointed us to a particular assignment. Our assignment is connected to the reason why God allowed us to be born. This scripture is directly talking about the Lord and His personal calling for Jeremiah the prophet. He tells Jeremiah that before he entered into His moment of time, He had already intended for Jeremiah to come and be a prophet. God is no respecter of persons; every person that comes into the earth has been created for a particular reason. Everything about you is used to influence your reason for being here. God is intentional and places us in times and generations because our calling fits the needs of the generation. You have been born for the time that you are needed the most. The fact that you are here on the earth at this particular time indicates that God has called you for such a time as this.

THE FIVE STAGES IN A LEADER'S EMERGENCE

I believe that everyone has leadership potential. I especially believe that when we come to know Christ, that He mantles us for a particular assignment. Although there are different variances related to how we lead and what we lead, the call to bring the gospel of Jesus Christ to the world is consistent. I believe every believer is a leader and that every believer has something special they have been called to do in their lifetime.

In knowing this truth, we must recognize that timing is everything. Knowing that you are called does not mean that it is the right season or time for you to walk in that calling. As a leader, I have witnessed people attempt to carry out their assignment prematurely. I have seen people step out and fail terribly because they did not grow through the process of development into purpose. People make the mistake of thinking that just because they are extremely gifted, that they are ready to walk in their assignment season. Gifts point you to assignment, but gifts don't indicate the season for the assignment. The only thing that indicates the right season is Heaven's endorsement and maturity. You must not skip the stages of development! How we grow through seasons will reveal to us if we are ready to embrace the next season. God wants to grow and prepare you for your destiny; He also wants to make sure that you finish strong and well.

I believe God has released potent gifts in the earth today. I believe because you are reading this book, you are one of those gifts. I am confident the Lord has great plans for you. If you are in your assignment, I believe that there is still more that you will do. Your story is still being written. God is getting ready to use you in a significant way in the earth. It is my goal to help you assess where you are in your season of emergence.

I love the conversation about destiny and assignment because your calling is not predicated on your age. I do believe that there are certain things that you should do in your youth, and other

I BELIEVE BECAUSE YOU ARE READING THIS BOOK, YOU ARE ONE OF THOSE GIFTS. I AM CONFIDENT THE LORD HAS GREAT PLANS FOR YOU.

things that should be done when you are older. There are certain things that will need a greater level of energy and there are other things that

will need more wisdom. However, as long as we have breath in our bodies, God has something for us to do. No matter what your age is or what season of life you are in, you have something to do. My admonishment is that you will not waste time. Make sure that you are hearing God and being obedient to His leading so that you aren't wasting time. I believe the enemy fills our life with distractions so that we waste time. He knows that we only have a certain amount of time to live on earth and he does all that he can to get you off course. It is his mission to get you distracted, sick, depressed, derailed, confused, discouraged and whatever else he does to cause us to waste time. You don't have time to waste; it is time for you to EMERGE!

I have had the privilege of serving in ministry for 20 years. I have also had extensive training in leadership and leadership development. I have seen over the years God use particular seasons to mature people as they are in the process of emerging. My wife, Brittany, and I have noticed in scripture various seasons in leadership development.

The first stage in leadership development is the season of invitation. This season is the time where God calls His people.

God always invites people to accept their destiny. The invitation season is time for self-discovery and passion.

> **MY ADMONISHMENT IS THAT YOU WILL NOT WASTE TIME.**
>
> **YOU DON'T HAVE TIME TO WASTE; IT IS TIME FOR YOU TO EMERGE!**

The second stage of leadership development is the season of apprenticeship. This season is where ones gifts are strengthened through education and serving. The apprenticeship season is the season for training.

The third stage in the journey to emerge is the season of validation and confirmation. This is the season where people begin to notice you and your talents. In this season, people start to get traction for what they are doing.

The fourth stages of development is the season of assignment. This is the season of destiny where we start to see our reason for being born. This is the season when your gift is at its height and you are at your best. This is the season that speaks to your reason for coming into the earth.

The fifth and final stage is the legacy season. This season is when someone has entered into the last leg of their life and they are called to train and impart. This is typically the season where a person is called to pour into the next generation.

Each of these seasons named are important and must be maximized. God is a God of order and process. Everything in the earth happens through season and process. You may be clear on your season, or you may be wondering how you can properly recognize your season. In the next chapters, I will spend more time unpacking how you can assess your seasons and provide you key strategies for being productive in each season.

CHAPTER 3

The Season of Invitation

As we discuss the seasons of development for leadership, we see the first season, and that is the season of invitation. In this season, the Lord reveals to an individual His intention for their life. Many times, people are walking along a path that is contrary to God's will for their life. Some people may not even be saved but God reveals His plan for their life by a divine revelation. There are different types of invitations and calls. In this chapter, I will discuss the different methods that God uses to reach His people.

The season of invitation is all about a person hearing the call and accepting it. This is the season of discovery, where God begins to inform you of your calling and purpose. The only way to fail in this season is to say no. The way to win in this season is to say yes to God. If you are in the season of invitation and you

> **THE SEASON INVITATION IS ALL ABOUT A PERSON HEARING THE CALL AND THEN ACCEPTING IT.**

are unsure of all that you are called to do, please do not allow your history or current thinking to build a picture in your mind of your future. God wants to blow your mind! God wants to perform His exceeding greatness for you and your life. In this season, you must ask God to give you the eyes to see.

I love the scripture in Ephesians 1:18 NIV, where Paul says,
"I pray that the eyes of your heart may be enlightened in order that you may know the hope to which he has called you, the riches of his glorious inheritance in his holy people."

This is a profound prayer. Paul is praying that these saints' eyes of the heart are opened so that they can know the plan that God has in store for them as believers. In the same way, I pray for you! I pray that you will have the spiritual awareness to understand all the great things that God has called you to do. My childhood pastor, Apostle William T. Broadous would say, "When God speaks, He expects a response." When the Lord speaks, make sure you give Him a yes.

God calls us in many different ways. In Genesis 12 we see the calling of Abram.

Now the Lord said to Abram, "Go from your country and your kindred and your father's house to the land that I will show you. And I will make of you a great nation, and I will bless you and make your name great, so that you will be a blessing. I will bless those who bless you, and him who dishonors you I will curse, and pin you all the families of the earth shall be blessed."3

Genesis 12:1-3 NIV

This verse indicates a divine calling where God is speaking audibly to Abram. God is inviting Abram into a new life and promising to bless him supernaturally. This calling is a divine call where God speaks audibly to Abram and gives him direct instruction regarding his calling and future. The audible voice of God is when one can literally hear what God is saying to them. Many times, the voice is profound and distinctive. God can also speak through prophetic dreams or prophetic insight.

Sometimes God will speak directly to you to inform you of what He desires for you to accomplish. God will speak audibly to make sure that you know it is His voice alone that is speaking to you. God spoke to Abram directly and informed him of what he wanted him to do. It was important for Abram to hear and trust God because apart of his calling was to establish what it means to walk in covenant with the God of creation. Many pioneers and builders will hear God audibly because of what they are called to build. Pioneers and builders must have the absolute confidence in God and His word to build something that has never been established on the earth before. This type of calling means that your faith may be tested, so you must know what the Lord has decreed.

This encounter is Abram's first experience with the God of creation. Based on his family's history and origin, Abram worshipped many different gods. It was necessary for God to speak audibly to get Abram to hear and then obey. God is willing to use whatever it takes to get you into a place of purpose and destiny. When God wants to get a point across to you, He will get your attention.

God can speak to us in different ways. Many times, people describe hearing from God through an inward witness. This can be a knowing, on the inside, of something that you are to do. Some may even call this an impression. The method of divine communication is when one feels from within what they should do. God will also use personal encounters like what we see with Moses and the burning bush. Let's look at the story.

> **GOD IS WILLING TO USE WHATEVER IT TAKES TO GET YOU INTO A PLACE OF PURPOSE AND DESTINY.**

Exodus 3:1-4 says,

> *"Now Moses was tending the flock of Jethro his father-in-law, the priest of Midian. And he led the flock to the back of the desert, and came to Horeb, the mountain of God. And the Angel of the Lord appeared to him in a flame of fire from the midst of a bush. So he looked, and behold, the bush was burning with fire, but the bush was not consumed. Then Moses said, "I will now turn aside and see this great sight, why the bush does not burn." So when the Lord saw that he turned aside to look, God called to him from the midst of the bush and said, "Moses, Moses!" And he said, "Here I am."*

One fascinating thought in this text is that Moses was tending the flock of his father-in-law. Moses encountered God in a season of service and humility. Moses grew up as the son of Pharaoh's daughter. He grew up as a royal Egyptian. All of his upbringing, experience, and education did not stop him from being faithful in serving. Moses' season with his father-in-law was a humble season, but it was a necessary one. Although he seemed to be in a place that lacked purpose, he was getting ready to encounter purpose.

Just because you are in a season that seems to be hard, low, or restrictive, does not mean that God does not have a call for you. God is sovereign and uses every season to prepare us for destiny. Everyone must have a beginning. Do not overlook or try to escape the process. God develops everything through process and time. Moses was in the wilderness tending the flock, but it was a season for him that was preparing him for his destiny. The key to every season that we endure is faithfulness.

DRIVING DREAM OR VISION

Joseph did not have an audible experience like Abraham or a supernatural theophany like Moses, but the Lord invited him into his calling through a prophetic dream and vision. In Genesis 37, we see that Joseph had two dreams. These dreams revealed the intent of God for Joseph's life. I believe these dreams opened Joseph up to receive what God had for him. I also believe that Joseph's dreams are what kept him through his slavery and imprisonment season. The Lord will show you a prophetic vision of who you are to become, to build faith, and instill a sense of hope in what the Lord will do in the future. Prophetic dreams are powerful tools for believers to receive the vision of God for their lives. Dreams open up our imagination to the limitless possibilities that the Lord has for us.

> **THE LORD WILL SHOW YOU A PROPHETIC VISION OF WHO YOU ARE TO BECOME, TO BUILD FAITH, AND TO INSTILL A SENSE OF HOPE IN WHAT THE LORD WILL DO IN THE FUTURE.**

PROPHETIC DECLARATION

God can invite you to His purpose for your life through prophetic declarations. Prophetic declaration happens when a person shares with you the word of the Lord regarding your calling and future. When these words are spoken, people are often not aware of the totality of their purpose or calling. God can use a prophet to speak His heart to you, and it sounds completely foreign to what you have thought or imagined. Many people mistakenly refute prophetic words because they think that prophetic words are intended only to confirm. It is not true. The prophetic word or prophetic declaration is spoken to bring us into the mind of God regarding our destiny. We can't limit prophetic declarations to confirm our experience because our vision and language could be limited in comprehending the mind of God regarding our life. Also, we may lack exposure, which can hinder our ability to see and perceive what God is decreeing. Therefore, when a prophetic word is spoken concerning your life, it is best to posture your heart to receive what the Lord is saying. 1 Samuel 10:1 gives us a brilliant example of how God can speak to us through prophetic declaration.

> *Then Samuel took a vial of oil and poured it on his head, and kissed him; he said, "The Lord has anointed you ruler over his people Israel. You shall reign over the people of the Lord and you will save them from the hand of their enemies all around. Now this shall be the sign to you that the Lord has anointed you ruler over his heritage:*
>
> 1 Samuel 10:1

THE PROPHETIC WORD OR PROPHETIC DECLARATION IS SPOKEN TO BRING US INTO THE MIND OF GOD REGARDING OUR DESTINY.

The Lord was getting ready to raise up a king for the nation of Israel. This nation had only known leaders who had judged them and the Lord being their head of state. The nation had never known a monarch in leadership over their nation. The Lord selected Saul and used the prophet, Samuel, to anoint him for the task at hand. Saul was on a mission to find his father's donkeys and had no clue that he would be anointed to be king of Israel. We can say that the thought could have possibly never crossed his mind because there had never been a human king of Israel before. Samuel's word was definitely a surprise to Saul, but it was the word of God.

31

It was through this prophetic encounter that Saul's life was changed forever. God used prophetic declaration to inform Saul of who he was to become. God will sometimes use a prophetic word to inform you of His intention for your life.

"Then the Spirit of the LORD will come upon you, and you will prophesy with them and be turned into another man."

1 Samuel 10:6

I love this! The prophetic word literally changed Saul and gave him what he needed to do the job at hand. Prophetic declarations have the power to shift you and change the trajectory of your life. God invited Saul to his destiny of kingship and equipped him to be a king.

King David came to leadership in a similar way. The Bible tells us of the story in 1 Samuel 16, it says the prophet Samuel is told by God to anoint another king of Israel. The Lord sent Samuel to a well-respected man's house, whose name was Jesse, to consecrate his son. Jesse had seven sons in total. Jesse called each of his sons, and the Lord did not call any of them to be the next king. After the prophet saw six of Jesse's sons, he asked if he had any others. The father responded by saying that he had a younger son who was in the wilderness keeping the sheep. Jesse overlooked David and did not regard him considerably for this great opportunity to be anointed by the prophet. David's role in his family was not one of prestige. He did not look like he should be a leader and probably did not think this could be his destiny. David was in the wilderness worshiping the Lord, protecting the flock, and serving his father. However, God's calling for his life was greater than sheep. The Lord knew exactly what he had called David to do. Neither David nor his family was aware of his potential, but that did not stop the Lord from anointing him. Although David was a lowly shepherd, he had a heart of a leader. You may feel like David, overlooked and rejected. You may also think that there is not much hope for you regarding purpose. You may also struggle with the idea of your purpose and potential. The Lord is not looking at your situation, thinking that He cannot use your story. The Lord looks at your life and sees all of the amazing things that He wants to do with it. David came into this truth after he encountered the Prophet Samuel.

The prophet Samuel represents the voice of God. Samuel was a fervent leader who God used to lead the people of Israel for many years. When he anointed David, he was endorsing David and sanctifying him for his assignment. The Lord will use prophetic voices and prophetic words to inform us of Heaven's intention for our lives. This is why it is important for us to receive the word of the Lord.

CALLING BY IMPARTATION

God uses impartation as a way of bringing His people into the knowledge of their assignment and calling. Romans 1:11 says, "For I long to see you, that I may impart to you some spiritual gift, so that you may be established" The word "impart" means to give a share of or to bestow. Paul is saying that he was to give the people of God a spiritual gift. It shows us that spiritual gifts can be given. Impartation can come through the laying on of hands, by direct mentorship or ministry. In 2 Timothy 1:6, Paul says to his spiritual son, Timothy, *"Therefore I remind you to stir up the gift of God which is in you through the laying on of my hands.* Paul is reminding his young disciple to fan the flame of the gifts imparted into him when he laid his hands on him. Paul understood that Timothy received his calling and giftedness through his impartation. When someone lays hands on you, they can impart gifts and anointings. There is a fascinating story found in the book of Numbers where the Lord allowed the anointing on Moses' life to come upon the elders and they prophesied.

> *So Moses went out and told the people the words of the Lord. And he gathered seventy men of the elders of the people and placed them around the tent. Then the Lord came down in the cloud and spoke to him, and took some of the Spirit that was on him and put it on the seventy elders. And as soon as the Spirit rested on them, they prophesied. But they did not continue doing it.*
>
> Numbers 11:24-25

The Lord took the grace that was on Moses and imparted that into the elders of Israel. It was an invitation to leadership. Moses' anointing came through process and development. However, these others received a portion of this anointing and were activated into a greater ministry level. It reveals to us the importance of mentorship and pastoring.

When you are connected with the right mentor or pastor, you can have graces and anointings unlocked in your life. The Lord will often place people in your life that will give you an example of your potential. These examples can help you to understand who you can become. You can receive your calling or understand your calling to leadership by the examples of people God places in your life.

Everyone should seek a good mentor and spiritual covering. We live in a day where people think they can do it alone, but there is something powerful about having great people who can mentor you. We see, biblically, that we can receive our leadership assignments through mentorship and training.

> *After the death of Moses the servant of the Lord, the Lord said to Joshua the son of Nun, Moses' assistant, "Moses my servant is dead. Now therefore arise, go over this Jordan, you and all this people, into the land that I am giving to them, to the people of Israel. Every place that the sole of your foot will tread upon I have given to you, just as I promised to Moses.*
>
> Joshua 1:1-4

The story of Joshua and how he came to be in leadership is fascinating. As discussed earlier in this chapter, Moses was called through a supernatural encounter with a burning bush. God used a supernatural sign to get his attention. However, Joshua got his calling to leadership through his position as a servant to Moses. Joshua assisted Moses for 40 years and was faithful in his call. It was in this service that the Lord promoted him to a position of leadership. God used his service to a man of God to be the place for Joshua to receive his assignment. Imagine if Joshua never submitted to serving Moses. Joshua would not have had the expertise and ability to lead the people of Israel. Sometimes God will place us in peculiar situations with various leaders to train us for His calling in our life. It is important that we don't miss the opportunity our season of service has for us.

I recall growing up in a semi-traditional Baptist church. My home church was progressive in theology but held to its foundational National Baptist roots in many ways. Through my young years, I had the opportunity of serving my pastor as an armor bearer. I know some people may not be familiar with this terminology, but an armor bearer supports the pastor in ministry. This support can vary depending upon the minister. Essentially, I was there to help the pastor with whatever he needed to minister. There were moments in service to my pastor that I hated! I hated them because they were at times laborious and arduous. I did not enjoy sitting through all the meetings, going to all the banquets, attending all the services, and participating in all the dinners. Honestly, much of my formative years, I spent them serving my pastor at my local church. Now, as a senior pastor of my church, I look back with great joy and gratitude to that season of service. It was in that season, that I learned almost everything I now know regarding ministry. At the time, I did not know who I would become, but the Lord placed me in the care of a leader who was an excellent example of leadership. I am confident that the season of ministry imparted something significant to me regarding my current season. You must remember that God can bring you into great clarity regarding your assignment through a season of service and mentorship.

CALLING THROUGH DIVINE SELECTION FAVOR AND GIFTEDNESS - ESTHER

I love the story of Esther in the Bible. Honestly, it is probably one of my favorite stories. The idea that God would make a poor orphan girl a queen is just amazing. This story always reminds me that God is never bothered by our circumstances and that the favor on our lives as His children is undeniable. The Bible tells us that Esther was favored by everyone in the palace, including the king. The king favored her so much that he made her a queen. Later on, there was a plot by one of the king's advisors to kill the Jews. Esther was made queen because of her beauty. She was not in this position because she was trained to be the head of state or council to her husband on foreign policy. Esther was in the palace because she was favored. Esther's uncle instructed her to speak up on behalf of her people and that she had come to the kingdom for that particular time.

> He says this in Esther 4:14 KJV, *"For if thou altogether holdest thy peace at this time, then shall there arise respite and deliverance to the Jews from another place, but thou and thy father's house shall be destroyed. And who knoweth whether thou art come to the kingdom for such a time as this?"*

Although Esther got her position based on her good looks and favor, the Lord used it to be a catalyst for her assignment. Thus, we are able to be invited into a season of leadership by divine selection, and giftedness.

I believe that the Lord is the giver of gifts. The Bible declares that our gifts will make room for us and bring us before great men. This is powerful. God can use your gifts to get you into the door, but the call of leadership and influence can sometimes be a by-product of the gift. Think about all of the artists and celebrities who have seriously impacted pop culture and even politics. People like Ronald Reagan, an actor turned politician and, Angelina Jolie, known for her philanthropic work, Shakira, and her work in building schools for her country, and Kim Kardashian and her prison reform efforts. These are some examples of people who gained influence through entertainment but used their success to champion causes beyond a gift. It is important to harness gifts and talents because the Lord can use them to set you on a course of greater influence. Esther's beauty got her in the door, but the invitation to leadership was a byproduct of the favor that she was granted. Your giftedness and favor can actually be an invitation to something more meaningful. DON'T MISS IT! Ask the Lord to reveal to you why you have been granted your influence.

> **YOUR GIFTEDNESS AND FAVOR CAN ACTUALLY BE AN INVITATION TO SOMETHING MORE MEANINGFUL.**

DIVINE DISRUPTION

Lastly, we can be invited into the season of leadership through divine disruption. We see this with Paul in Acts 9. Saul was on the road to Damascus to continue his vicious campaign to persecute the Christians of his day. He was set on bringing destruction to the church, and he had the authority to do it. On his way, he was interrupted by God. The Lord revealed himself to Saul, and it changed his life forever. There are some people who are knuckleheads, and they don't get free unless something crazy happens to them. These are the people who have crazy stories of salvation and conversions. God uses supernatural intervention to reveal his power to people and bring them into a greater understanding of their life assignment.

> *Then Saul, still breathing threats and murder against the disciples of the Lord, went to the high priest and asked letters from him to the synagogues of Damascus, so that if he found any who were of the Way, whether men or women, he might bring them bound to Jerusalem. As he journeyed he came near Damascus, and suddenly a light shone around him from heaven. Then he fell to the ground, and heard a voice saying to him, "Saul, Saul, why are you persecuting Me?" And he said, "Who are You, Lord?" Then the Lord said, "I am Jesus, whom you are persecuting. It is hard for you to kick against the goads." So he, trembling and astonished, said, "Lord, what do You want me to do?" Then the Lord said to him, "Arise and go into the city, and you will be told what you must do." And the men who journeyed with him stood speechless, hearing a voice but seeing no one. Then Saul arose from the ground, and when his eyes were opened he saw no one. But they led him by the hand and brought him into Damascus. And he was three days without sight, and neither ate nor drank.*
>
> Acts 9:1-9

This experience was extreme. I believe that the Lord did this with Paul because he was so dedicated to his personal ideals. He could not have been talked out or convinced that he was not right regarding his conviction against Christianity. Saul was a stubborn personality. The Lord, in His sovereignty, knew Saul's temperament. He knew it because that's how He created him. God had a purpose in mind. God allowed him to grow in the Jewish faith and to matriculate through his religious education. God desired to use Paul's scholarship to advance the gospel.

There are some people that only the Lord can reach. You may even have people in your life that seems to be so hard-headed and far away. You may have a loved one that you can see their potential. But they seemed not to be coming into faith any time soon. My encouragement is for you to not give up on them as you pray for them. Continue to press in regarding them and their acceptance of their call. Please remember that God knows how to reach His children. In the same way that God got ahold of Paul, He will get ahold of your loved one.

KNOWING THE CALL OF THE LORD

When I speak of "the call," I am referring to God's invitation into one's assignment and destiny. I believe that God has a call for everyone! Every believer has a particular calling or assignment that they are to do to advance the kingdom of God and impact the world. Unfortunately, many people disregard and minimize their assignments. It happens when people are busy comparing themselves to other people. It is a freeing thing to realize that

God gave all His children a charge to keep and that His definition of success is different from ours. God views success by completed assignments; man equates success with influence and wealth. We must not allow anything keep us from walking in our assignment.

People run from their calling all the time. I have met and counseled people who acted as if they did not know their call while deep down they knew. One of the main hindrances to people moving forward is fear. Remember, fear is not of the Lord. Fear is a tool of the enemy to keep people from obtaining greatness. The enemy is dedicated to limiting us from reaching our potential. This is why God uses different ways to reach His people. In this chapter, I have named a few examples of how God invites His people to their position as leaders. No matter how you have been called, you must always keep your encounter true to your heart.

> **WE MUST NOT ALLOW ANYTHING KEEP US FROM WALKING IN OUR ASSIGNMENT.**

> **THE ENEMY IS DEDICATED TO LIMITING US FROM REACHING OUR POTENTIAL.**

Apostle William T. Broadous would always say, "When God speaks, he expects a response." Therefore, when God speaks to us, it is important that we respond appropriately. We see great examples of this throughout scripture.

When the Lord revealed Himself to Abram and told him about His place for his life, the Bible tells us that Abram responded to God by building an altar.

> *Then the Lord appeared to Abram and said, "To your descendants I will give this land." And there he built an altar to the Lord, who had appeared to him.*
>
> Genesis 12:7

This altar represents sacrifice and worship. This altar also served as a memorial of Abram's encounter with God. Abram's response to God was with worship and prayer. We see in Genesis 13:3-4 That Abram returns to the place where he built an altar and called on the Lord. When we encounter God, we need to build an altar in our hearts. This is the place that we can pull strength from while we are growing through different seasons of life.

As you accept your call to leadership, many things will make you want to quit and throw in the towel. However, if you create a space in your heart of worship and ponder on the word of God, you can encourage yourself. As we develop, there are times where the word of God feels far and rare. There are other times where we second guess if what we heard and experienced is true. The Bible tells us in Luke 2:19 how Mary, the mother of Jesus, "pondered" in her heart what was to come. When

IT IS IMPORTANT TO ACCEPT THE CALL AND NOT TRY TO RUSH THE SEASON.

Jesus was an infant and Mary witnessed all of the happenings around His birth and presence, she processed what was going on personally. Mary took it all in. It is important to accept the call and not try to rush the season. While you are in the season of invitation and you feel called or feel burdened, take these feelings to the Lord and wait on the Lord to lead your steps and direction on what is to come next. All that you do, please do not make the mistake of rushing into purpose and stepping out before your time. Enjoy the season that you have, and let God perfect everything concerning you.

CHAPTER 4

Apprenticeship Season

I will never forget when the Lord called me into ministry. It was the evening of my church's annual Children's Day. Every year, our church would host various annual Sunday programs that would highlight a particular group. Such as our annual Women's Day, Men's Day, Usher Day, and Children's Day. I always loved this time of year because our church did an excellent job of making church fun and engaging.

The children were responsible for all the various aspects of our Sunday experiences. We would also have various guest ministers that preached messages to the children. Those that knew me as a child, would tell you that I was the definition of a church kid. I was at church all of the time and I loved it. One particular Children's Day was extremely special to me. I remember the speaker sharing their testimony of being called to ministry when they were a child and I felt openness to the Lord for Him to use me if He desired. I was nine years old at the time so I could not properly articulate my feeling towards the Lord—all I knew was that I was open to Him.

That evening I was home watching the 70s TV show, "The Jefferson's" and then an unexplainable presence entered my room. I did not see anything, all I felt was a heaviness that entered into my room. At that moment, I heard, "I have called you to ministry." Honestly, words are not adequate enough to explain this experience. I now know that what I experienced in my room was the glory of God, and God used His glory to reveal His reality to me and to let me know that there was something significant that He had called me to do.

I was filled with emotion and joy and began to weep in the presence of God. I called for my parents and told them my experience and they were equally amazed. My mother told me that I should talk to my pastor about my encounter. I remember meeting with Apostle Broadus, telling him what happened and that I was called to do ministry. He was excited because he said that he had known that God had a special plan for my life. He looked at me and said, "Son, you will now be under my tutelage." This began a 14-year journey of training and preparation for ministry under Apostle Broadus' leadership.

After this conversation, he brought me in very close to him in ministry. I would eventually become his armor bearer, church office worker, praise and worship leader, assistant to the pastor, a conference planner, usher, and anything else the church needed.

The second stage of the emergence process is the apprenticeship season, where one serves under someone else to be trained. God is a God of mentorship and training. Whenever one is ready to emerge or come to a higher level of operation, God always assigns people to mentor and coach them to be perfected in their leadership. This season can be compared to the "wilderness." It is the season where people feel the most stretched. We see in scripture that the Lord uses the wilderness to train His people for their assignment. The wilderness is a place of development and cultivation. It is important for leaders to be cultivated beyond just giftedness. Many people are charismatic and gifted, but it is evident that they lack cultivation. My pastor used to take me everywhere he went. He did this to train me for what ministry looked like. One particular time, I was at a pastoral banquet. I was approximately 15 years old, and I was at a table with many different pastors. I remember my pastor correcting me a few times on the proper etiquette of addressing senior leaders and how I should conduct myself as a man of God. My pastor was cultivating me and training me for my future as a senior pastor. This season gives us the opportunity to grow and develop.

First, you will have the call, then you are given a mentor or person to train you. Everyone does not have a direct person, but sometimes it can be a season of training. Sometimes the person is distant, and they can train you from afar. This training can be through teachings, research, books, and article writings. There may not be one person who is training directly, but it can be a season of training. In this season, God always assigns people who can help to direct you. It can even happen under terrible leaders and unhealthy organizations. I have heard countless horror stories of people learning from bad examples. The truth is that training is necessary. I believe with all my heart, that when God calls you, He will give you mentors and examples to assist you in your development.

One of the things that I have seen with many emerging leaders is that they discredit and disregard God's people directly in their lives. It happens for several reasons. One of the biggest reasons that I have found is that the

THE TRUTH IS THAT TRAINING IS NECESSARY.

emerging leader has a vision that exceeds the examples of their mentor and teachers. It is appropriate because we are to go from glory to glory. Therefore, we should improve with every generation. The issue arises when we dishonor those that have been set in our lives to teach us. We must be sure that we honor the people in our lives who are called to assist us in reaching our destiny. God does not make mistakes; God is intentional and knows the steps we are to take.

Another major concern that I have for emerging leaders is that many people do not value the season of being processed. We live in a time of quick turnaround and a micro-wave mindset. This is the mindset that everything should happen quickly. People get a prophetic word or receive a calling

WE MUST BE SURE THAT WE HONOR THE PEOPLE IN OUR LIVES WHO ARE CALLED TO ASSIST US IN REACHING OUR DESTINY.

for something, and they think they can immediately start doing their assignment. One time, I gave a young man a word in my church regarding his potential for ministry. I intended to encourage him on what I saw in him and get his faith aligned with his potential. The next day, he asked me if he could preach for a

Sunday service. He heard a word and thought that he should be up to preach. In our church, there is a process for training leaders and ministry gifts; this young man wanted to skip our process and start preaching. Many people are just like this. They want to skip the process that God has laid out for them to be equipped for their season of leadership.

In Matthew 3, we see Jesus being baptized by John the Baptist. This passage shows us a beautiful picture of Jesus being affirmed as the son of God and the Holy Spirit descending as a dove to confirm that Jesus was the Messiah.

> *"And when Jesus was baptized, immediately he went up from the water, and behold, the heavens were opened to him, and he saw the Spirit of God descending like a dove and coming to rest on him; and behold, a voice from heaven said, "This is my beloved Son, with whom I am well pleased." (Matthew 4:1) Then Jesus was led up by the Spirit into the wilderness to be tempted by the devil.*
> Matthew 3:16-17, 4:1-1

The Bible says something interesting in Matthew 4:1. It says that the Holy Spirit led Jesus into the wilderness to be tempted by the devil. This word "tempted" speaks of being tested. When the Lord speaks prophetically over our lives, He then assigns us to a training and testing season. In scripture, we see that the Lord affirmed Jesus, but that Jesus did not go directly into His ministry. Following His baptism, Jesus went into a season of further consecration and process. His season of process was the wilderness. Please note that the wilderness season can vary for everyone. In addition to the wilderness season, there is the hidden season. These seasons can be separate or together however, this part of the journey is all for development.

The Bible says that the Holy Spirit led Jesus into the wilderness. Jesus was hidden in His adolescent years. Luke 2 gives the story of Jesus staying behind in the temple after His parents had started their journey home. His parents got worried because Jesus was not in their caravan. They went back to look for Him and found Him sitting with the Rabbi in the temple.

> *So when they saw Him, they were amazed; and His mother said to Him, "Son, why have you done this to us? Look, your father and I have sought you anxiously." And He said to them, "Why did you seek Me? Did you not know that I must be about My Father's business?" But they did not understand the statement which He spoke to them. Then He went down with them and came to Nazareth and was subject to them, but His mother kept all these things in her heart. And Jesus increased in wisdom and stature, and in favor with God and men.*
>
> Luke 2:48-52

In this verse, Jesus is 12 years old, and He is aware of His calling and who He was. He was knowledgeable of the scriptures and impressed the Rabbis. However, it was not His time to emerge. When seeing Jesus in Matthew 4, He is 30 years old. This means that Jesus started His formal ministry nearly 20 years after this occasion in Luke 2. The Bible says that Jesus increased in wisdom and stature and favor with God and men. This 20-year gap was the time that Jesus grew. Jesus was not ready to be the Savior on the cross at this time; Jesus had to increase in knowledge and maturity. The Bible says that Jesus' trade was carpentry. We know that His father, Joseph, was a carpenter, and Jesus had to learn His father's trade. He probably had to serve him as an apprentice. Jesus needed time to develop and grow into His assignment.

In Galatians 4, this scripture talks about "the fullness of time." This scripture is referring to the coming of the Messiah. Jesus came to the earth at the fullness of time. We see at the fall of man in Genesis 3 a prophetic reference to Jesus. The entire Old Testament is a timeline to reveal to us the lineage of Jesus and His ancestral history. There are numerous prophecies in the Old Testament that foretell the coming of Jesus. Through it all, Jesus had to come on the scene at the right time. With Jesus' birth, the earth had to wait 30 years for Jesus to be equipped to be the ruling king of the cross. You will be launched into ministry and in your call in the fullness of time. This process should not be mismanaged; it should be embraced with gratitude because God is making something great in you as you wait for your time.

The apprenticeship season is all about education and development. I cannot tell you how many people my wife and I counseled, who shared their big dreams and visions, that lacked an education plan. It is always amazing when someone talks about their assignment, and they do not have a clue on the process that it will take to excel in that field. Now please do not stop reading or skip this chapter because I am talking about education. I know everyone has had different experiences with formal education. Some people are natural students, and others struggle a little more. To be honest, I am one of those people who have struggled through school. I did not necessarily struggle to make solid grades, but school seemed too restrictive. I desired to be freer and to learn by experience as opposed to the formal classroom setting in my process. I believe that formal education is not for everyone. I also believe that formal schooling is designed for a certain type of learners and limits the cultivation of brilliance and creativity for others. With all this said, there is still a need for leaders to be educated.

> **THE APPRENTICESHIP SEASON IS ALL ABOUT EDUCATION AND DEVELOPMENT.**

When I speak of education, I am talking about preparation and training. Your educational process should be congruent with your place of calling and assignment. If you are called to entrepreneurship, you should be educated in the particular market you are launching into and the strategies to succeed. If you are called to arts and entertainment, you should find ways to master that craft and be the best in that field. Certain areas do not require a degree, but it may require certification, or other areas require formal education. I have heard many people talk about their calling to politics and policy, but they have no training to support it. The apprenticeship season is the time to learn and grow. As you are processing through your assignment, it is essential to chart your educational course. If formal training is required, do not allow anything to detour you from qualifying yourself for where you have been called. It is important to remember that God is the one who called you, and He will give you the grace you need to complete the assignment. Many times people take God out of the equation for educa-tion. If the Lord has called you to a field of influence, this means He will grace you to endure whatever pro-cess it takes to get there. Please do not take on the idea that

IF FORMAL TRAINING IS REQUIRED, DO NOT ALLOW ANYTHING TO DETOUR YOU FROM QUALIFYING YOURSELF FOR WHERE YOU HAVE BEEN CALLED.

you do not need earthly endorsements or credentials because you have Heaven's blessing. Yes, it is absolutely true that your calling indeed comes with the acceptance of Heaven, but having the ac-knowledgment of peers and other professionals gives credibility. The Lord wants His people to be the best because we represent the best.

In my experience, much of the mentors that I have gained have been through my formal education. My wife, Brittany, and I met in college at Oral Roberts University (ORU). She was an education major, and I was a business major. I had the privilege of working for the Dean of the School of Education, Dr. Kimberly Boyd. This woman was excellent in every way possible. She and her husband were both employed by the university, and they pastored a local church. I am honored to say that I grew pretty close to this couple during my time at ORU. Brittany also grew from a close relationship with Dr. Boyd. She developed more of a mentor and mentee relationship. My wife would spend days with Dr. Boyd, going with her to all of her appointments. She would see Dr. Boyd, lead the School of Education, lecture a class, go to funerals, counsel students, be an attentive mother and a loving wife. Brittany would plan workshops for Dr. Boyd and other events to help mentor other young ladies.

During this time, my wife's only responsibility was to be a student. As a student, she saw a direct example of what she was called to do and was an eyewitness to an example of her potential. Although their exchange was not necessarily deep, there was something that was transferred in this relationship. It is hard to believe that my wife and I walked the halls of ORU fourteen years ago. Honestly, there is so much that has changed since then. Every day, I witness my wife balance so much. She is a school director, pastor, consultant, community leader, mentor, mother, daughter, and wife. Brittany is a woman of grace and excellence. In many moments, I can see the impartation of Dr. Boyd. My wife would not have had this example if she had not said yes to God and pursued her formal education. As the quote by Tae Te Ching says, "When the student is ready, the teacher will appear. When the student is truly not ready, the teacher will disappear.

As developing leaders, we must embrace the season of being trained and serving under seasoned leaders to be cultivated. We see many stories in the Bible regarding training and mentorship. We see Moses and Joshua, Eli and Samuel, David and Saul, Elijah and Elisha, Ruth and Naomi, Mordecai and Esther, Jesus and the

Disciples, and Paul and Timothy. These are just a few examples of how God uses mentors to equip us in walking in destiny. Mentors can speak the language that activates the mentee's faith in walking in their destiny.

> 1Corinthians 4:15 says,
> *"For though you might have ten thousand instructors in Christ, yet you do not have many fathers; for in Christ Jesus I have begotten you through the gospel."*

This verse says that we have many teachers. Teachers can be a mentor or a coach. These people can be ones that you learn from through many different vehicles. Mentors and coaches can be motivational speakers, pastors, industry leaders, YouTubers, authors, podcasters, and many more outlets that you can pull information from. It is healthy to find teachers to help you in your profession. I encourage you to seek out people that can pour into your life. You can have teachers that you never physically or personally encounter. I know countless stories of people who have benefited and strengthened through the teachings and writings of respected industry leaders. The apprenticeship season is one's opportunity to learn and glean all that one can. It is the season where a person's only responsibility is to be a student and a servant.

As I reflect back on my journey, I can't help but think about my college years. I did not know during that time, but those years were some of the best years of my life. I had no responsibilities and my only task was to get good grades and graduate from school. The whole concept of being away from home studying was powerful. As a student all my needs were met and I had the freedom to being a young adult away from home. One of the biggest regrets that I have now is that I did not take full advantage of that season. Please don't get me wrong, I enjoyed my experience, but there are some things that I wish I could have done different in that season. One of my major regrets is not studying abroad. Although I love to travel and experiencing culture, I wish I would have taken the opportunity to be a foreign exchange student in a different country. I also regret not getting my MBA right after finishing business school. My school offered a one-year accelerated MBA program that I should have completed. These are two examples of opportunities that my college season offered me that required my participation then. Unfortunately, my current season doesn't afford me the luxury to pick and study in a different country. This is an example of the importance of taking full advantage of what a season offers. In the apprenticeship season, it is the time to be a sponge and learn all that you can. It is important to get as many teachers, mentors, and tutors as possible, because the day to walk in destiny is coming and how you process through the season of training will indicate your success.

1 Corinthians 4:15 also shows us that although we have many teachers, we don't have many fathers. This primary scripture, indicates that the concept of spiritual fathering is extracted. A spiritual father cultivates and raises up spiritual children to walk in their calling or destiny. A spiritual father or mother essentially has the ability to birth their spiritual children in reference to their ministry and calling. I am saddened by how the concept of

spiritual fathering and mothering has been abused. This concept is not just for a title, but it represents one of the highest levels of impartation. A spiritual father has the spiritual authority by God to raise up sons. Spiritual fathers and mothers are people that have a direct coalition to one's development. A true spiritual father will see your potential and help bring it out. In the secular community, it represents mentorship and development. A spiritual father should have the ability to see beyond their son. Spiritual fathers should also have the resources and knowledge to launch their spiritual children into successful ministries and careers. Spiritual fathering is not about being served but serving spiritual children to ensure they have what they need to thrive alone. A true father or mother will have the capacity to see potential in their spiritual children and raise it up. Spiritual parents are assigned to help their spiritual sons and daughters to hear God's voice.

We see this example with the young prophet Samuel and Eli. When Samuel first heard God call his name, he thought it was his spiritual father calling him. Eli had to instruct Samuel on how to hear God and respond to Him. Many times God clarifies and defines these types of relationships in the apprenticeship season. Many people seek their spiritual father and mother based on a person's notoriety and success. It is important to remember that this particular relationship is divine and is orchestrated by the Holy Spirit. When the Lord has placed you with a leader that can speak into your life, see your potential, impart into you, you must not fight that but lean into it and submit. It is perfectly okay to seek out these types of relationships, but it is imperative not to overlook the people in your life that God assigns to raise you up.

My favorite example of this exchange is Elijah and Elisha. Let's take a look at this passage found in 1 Kings 19:15-21 KJV

And the Lord said to him, "Go, return on your way to the wilderness of Damascus. And when you arrive, you shall anoint Hazael to be king over Syria. And Jehu the son of Nimshi you shall anoint to be king over Israel, and Elisha the son of Shaphat of Abel-meholah you shall anoint to be prophet in your place. And the one who escapes from the sword of Hazael shall Jehu put to death, and the one who escapes from the sword of Jehu shall Elisha put to death. Yet I will leave seven thousand in Israel, all the knees that have not bowed to Baal, and every mouth that has not kissed him." So he departed from there and found Elisha, the son of Shaphat, who was plowing with twelve yoke of oxen in front of him, and he was with the twelfth. Elijah passed by him and cast his cloak upon him. And he left the oxen and ran after Elijah and said, "Let me kiss my father and my mother, and then I will follow you." And he said to him, "Go back again, for what have I done to you?" And he returned from following him and took the yoke of oxen and sacrificed them and boiled their flesh with the yokes of the oxen and gave it to the people, and they ate. Then he arose and went after Elijah and assisted him.

We see in verse 17 that the Lord speaks to Elijah and tells him to anoint Elisha to be his successor in this prophetic ministry. God shows us here how succession should be in the mind of every leader. It is the responsibility of the leader to anoint and impart to those that they have been called to minister after them. Seasoned leaders should be imparting and raising up their successors. Unfortunately, we are seeing this failure today. Many senior leaders are not duplicating themselves or raising up the next generation. We will talk about this concept more later in the chapters to come.

In verse 19, Elijah finds Elisha plowing with twelve yokes of oxen. Elisha was found working his business. Elijah sees him and then throws his cloak on him. The Bible doesn't tell us that Elijah said anything to Elisha; all he did was place his mantle on him. It was a prophetic act. Elisha was working a regular job and was not walking to his fullest potential. It does not tell us that Elisha even knew that he had a prophetic call. Elisha was just living. Elijah's cloak represented his calling, ministry, and

> **SEASONED LEADERS SHOULD BE IMPARTING AND RAISING UP THEIR SUCCESSORS.**

position with God. Elijah casting this cloak on Elisha was a sign of Elisha's potential and possible future. Sometimes we can see our potential through other leaders. Elijah was showing his future mentee that he could walk in the same power that he walked him without words. God used Elijah to open Elisha's understanding of who he could become.

In verse 20, we see Elisha leaving the oxen and running after Elijah. All the prophet Elijah did was give him a glimpse of Elisha's potential, but it was up to Elisha to perceive and understand this significant action. Thank God Elisha did. Elisha saw God's plan for his life and was willing to give up what he was doing and chase after it. The oxen represents Elisha's business and his occupation. The Bible says that he left his occupation and ran after Elijah. He left his earthly job to chase after his spiritual assignment. When Elisha saw and had this encounter, he went after his mentor. Elisha was willing to stop what he was doing to receive the deposit for his future. I have heard many people talk about how they cannot pursue their dreams because they are stuck for some reason or another. You will not emerge if you are not willing to sacrifice. When the Lord is calling you to something deeper and better, don't allow anything to keep you from receiving what you need to for your future.

Elisha served as Elijah's apprentice for six years. Elisha was committed to this season. The Bible tells us that Elisha sacrificed his oxen business. In pursuit of his destiny, he destroyed his means of making money. He dedicated himself fully to purpose. Please hear me, I'm not saying that people should be reckless, but I am saying that when God calls us to do something, we should be willing to do whatever it takes to prepare ourselves for that assignment. Sometimes this looks like going back to school; it could also look like doing an internship or joining a mentorship program. The objective is to follow God and pursue His future for your life. One thing to note is that God told Elijah to anoint Elisha, but Elisha was not formerly anointed in this scripture. His anointing came as a response to his service to Elijah. We can receive impartation through service. If you are seeking to grow in an industry, and you see an individual doing well in that field, serve them and learn from them. The apprenticeship season is not a forever assignment, but it is the time to learn and grow.

LESSONS FROM ELISHA:

One, Elisha understood the spiritual transaction between him and Elijah. He respected the mantle on Elijah's life. Secondly, Elisha ran after his mentor. He positioned himself in a position to receive from his mentor. And Thirdly, Elisha, disconnected from his past. Elisha said goodbye to his family and old life to move to his future.

If you identify yourself in this season of waiting, please make it a point to pass the test. This season is all about passing the test and making sure that you are set up well for your future. It is important to find a mentor or teacher. Once you find that person be faithful to serve them in whatever possible way. While you are serving, make sure you learn and grow. Do not ever waste the season by being too familiar or casual. When you are in the presence of a God-ordained mentor, you must recognize that there is a spiritual exchange taking place. Learn everything that you can. While you are in this season, please remember that your turn is coming. Do not be anxious or overly zealous. Allow yourself to be processed in time. The main objective in this season is to pass the test of the season.

FIND A MENTOR OR TEACHER.

CHAPTER 5

The Validation Season

So far we have discussed two phases of maturation in leadership development. We started off talking about the invitation. In the season of invitation, we come into an understanding of our call and God's design for our life. This is the time where future leaders discover who they are and what they were born to do. After this phase, we talked about the phase of being an apprentice and student. The priority of this phase is learning and serving. This chapter is dedicated to the 3rd phase in the process and that is season of validation.

Validation is defined as the action of checking or providing the validity or accuracy of something. Another definition is the action of making or declaring something legally or officially acceptable. In terms of leadership, the season of validation is when an individual is transitioning from an apprentice into a leader. During this time, the Lord allows one to be noticed for their competencies regarding their assignment. This is also the time when people begin to endorse the validity of the call on one's life. It is important to recognize that this is not the time when one walks into the fullness of their leadership, but the moment when they begin to grow in their influence.

In Genesis 3 we see the first Messianic prophecy. This is a prophetic word that speaks of Jesus and His assignment in the earth. The entire Old Testament is essentially a timeline that details the lineage of the coming of Jesus. We see there are actually over 300 Old Testament prophecies that speak of Jesus. He came to earth thousands of years after He was prophesied to.

> *Then Jesus came from Galilee to John at the Jordan to be baptized by him. And John tried to prevent Him, saying, "I need to be baptized by You, and are You coming to me?" But Jesus answered and said to him, "Permit it to be so now, for thus it is fitting for us to fulfill all righteousness." Then he allowed Him. When He had been baptized, Jesus came up immediately from the water; and behold, the heavens were opened to Him, and He saw the Spirit of God descending like a dove and alighting upon Him. And suddenly a voice came from heaven, saying, "This is My beloved Son, in whom I am well pleased."*
>
> Matthew 3:13-17

We see Jesus being baptized in this passage. He goes to His cousin, John, to be baptized right before He launches His public ministry. As stated earlier, the Old Testament is full of prophecies regarding the Messiah. Essentially every generation since Adam has been in expectation of the coming of Jesus to save the world. We see Him born, and then we see Him again, at the age of 12, at the temple. After seeing Him in the temple, we do not see Jesus again until He is an adult. I believe that those years were pertinent for Jesus' development as the Savior of the world. Jesus gets baptized right before He turns the world upside down through His ministry. The Bible states that when Jesus was baptized the Heavens opened to Him, the Holy Spirit descended on Him, and the Lord spoke and said, "This is my beloved Son, with whom I am well pleased." This was Heaven's endorsement. Jesus' baptism is the official announcement of His ministry. The Holy Spirit descending on Him represents the anointing of God. It was the moment when Jesus was anointed to serve God's people as the Messiah. When Jesus came out of the water, the Lord spoke from Heaven and validated His relationship to Him and that He was pleased with Him. Jesus had to be validated by Heaven before He could move into His ministry.

Acts 13:2-3 tells us the story of when the disciples were worshiping the Lord and the Holy Spirit told them to set apart Barnabas and Paul for the work of ministry. The disciples then laid hands on them and sent them off. Paul and Barnabas had already been involved in ministry before this encounter. This was the validation from Heaven to release them into their destiny. Every gift must be tested and proven before it can be released into the world for maximum impact. There is no exception to this principle. Again, a gift must be tested and proven before its ready to be revealed to a world of influence. I have witnessed many people step out before they have been tried and proven and the results are always disastrous. My word of caution to anyone who is unwilling to go through the process of maturation that has been laid before them is to SLOW DOWN. The objective in all that we do is to finish well and strong.

Sometimes validations can come immediately after one's activation or announcement of assignment. This typically happens when people have already been active in their call without endorsement. These are people who serve in various areas without knowing that it may be a call for them. These people volunteer their time in ministry or with organizations. They are people who are faithful serving in an area just because they love

MY WORD OF CAUTION TO ANYONE WHO IS UNWILLING TO GO THROUGH THE PROCESS OF MATURATION THAT HAS BEEN LAID BEFORE THEM IS TO SLOW DOWN.

it. I've witnessed it with my mother. For as long as I can remember, my mother has served in women's ministry. She planned women conferences, hosted gatherings, preached for women services, mentored young women, and was a spiritual mother to many. After at least 20 years of faithful service in ministry, she announced that she was called to be a preacher. After her announcement, she was quickly ordained and released into formal ministry. The speed of her process was due to her being faithful in developing her gift for years. The title and ordination was just the icing on the cake.

The key to all of these various steps is in the process. The idea is this; when we walk in the spiritual order, we are to be validated, and anointed before we emerge as a "full gift" or leader. We must not expect to walk in assignments because we think that we are ready to start. Jesus' baptism began a 40-day journey in the wilderness to be tempted. In the previous chapter, we talked about how the apprenticeship season was the time when we have to pass the test. In your season of validation, there are also times of testing. This testing is different. It's not a testing of ability, it's testing of maturity, responsibility, and readiness.

Then Jesus was led up by the Spirit into the wilderness to be tempted by the devil. And after fasting forty days and forty nights, he was hungry. And the tempter came and said to him, "If you are the Son of God, command these stones to become loaves of bread." But he answered, "It is written, 'Man shall not live by bread alone, but by every word that comes from the mouth of God.'" Then the devil took him to the holy city and set him on the pinnacle of the temple and said to him, "If you are the Son of God, throw yourself down, for it is written, "'He will command his angels concerning you,' and "'On their hands they will bear you up, lest you strike your foot against a stone.'" Jesus said to him, "Again it is written, 'You shall not put the Lord your God to the test.'" Again, the devil took him to a very high mountain and showed him all the kingdoms of the world and their glory. And he said to him, "All these I will give you, if you will fall down and worship me." Then Jesus said to him, "Be gone, Satan! For it is written, "'You shall worship the Lord your God and him only shall you serve.'" Then the devil left him, and behold, angels came and were ministering to him.

Matthew 4:1-11

In this chapter of Matthew, we see Jesus being tempted by the enemy. Jesus was actually tempted three different times. The first temptation was Satan telling Jesus to turn stones to bread. *And the tempter came and said to him, "If you are the Son of God, command these stones to become loaves of bread." But he answered, "It is written, 'Man shall not live by bread alone, but by every word that comes from the mouth of God.* This first temptation was the temptation of the lust of flesh. Jesus was called to an intense time of consecration to prepare Him for His earthly assignment. The enemy tried to distract Him with substance to feed His flesh and natural appetite. It was also a temptation for Jesus to use His power to make this stone into bread essentially using His giftedness to satisfy His flesh. This temptation would hinder Jesus from being able to endure the cross. His main assignment was to endure the cross and to die in the flesh. If He could not withstand food, He wouldn't be able to endure the agony of the cross. Jesus had to conquer His appetite to be able to conquer death by dying on the cross. Jesus responded to Satan with the word of God saying, "Man does not live by bread alone, but by the words that come from the mouth of God." Jesus was fasting to tap into a greater level of spiritual strength. Bread represents natural nourishment, but the word of God represents spiritual nourishment.

Many times, we must conquer the small things in our lives to be positioned for greater. I am always amazed when I hear people talk about their great dreams and plans but refuse to employ discipline in their everyday life. These people speak of starting a business but never see it off the ground. Or people that have conversations regarding their major in college without ever taking a class. The validation season proves that one has what it takes to not cave in during temptation. Just think about all of the great people who have fallen because they could not bring their flesh into alignment with the will of God. Jesus passing this test showed His ability to deny His flesh to pursue a higher call.

> **WE MUST CONQUER THE SMALL THINGS IN OUR LIVES TO BE POSITIONED FOR THE GREATER.**

The next temptation that we see deals with a difference set of issues that leaders must be sure to avoid. Matthew 4:5-7 says,

> *"Then the devil took him to the holy city and set him on the pinnacle of the temple and said to him, "If you are the Son of God, throw yourself down, for it is written, "'He will command his angels concerning you,' and "'On their hands they will bear you up, lest you strike your foot against a stone.'" Jesus said to him, "Again it is written, 'You shall not put the Lord your God to the test.'"*

This temptation was dealing with human pride and self-exaltation. Satan was trying to have the Lord make Himself a public spectacle. It was the temptation to make His calling about Himself and not the people that He was called to serve. Jesus' gifts, position, and assignment was for the benefit of God's kingdom. Jesus' mission was to be the Savior of the world. He had the power to command the armies of Heaven and they would have responded by His word. The temple was a central meeting place for Jews in Jesus' day. There were always people at the temple. Satan was trying to get Jesus to make a scene and show how great He was. Jesus had to pass this test because of what was to come in the future. He is the Lamb of God and did not come into the earth to lead a boastful ministry. He came to serve the world humbly. This very action would have changed the narrative of His ministry. As you are preparing to emerge, you will be tempted to make your assignment about you. This temptation attempts to cause you to forsake the fact that your calling has been given to you by the Lord for His people. Many people allow their talent to get the best of them. Remember that your gifts have been given to you to serve the Lord and benefit the world.

> **AS YOU ARE PREPARING TO EMERGE, YOU WILL BE TEMPTED TO MAKE YOUR ASSIGNMENT BE ABOUT YOU.**

The third temptation deals with the lust of the eyes.

Again, the devil took him to a very high mountain and showed him all the kingdoms of the world and their glory. And he said to him, "All these I will give you, if you will fall down and worship me." Then Jesus said to him, "Be gone, Satan! For it is written, "'You shall worship the Lord your God and him only shall you serve.'"

Then the devil left him, and behold, angels came and were ministering to him.

Matthew 4:8-11

Satan promised to give all the kingdoms and glories of the world to Jesus if he would bow down to him and worship. We read in scripture that through the cross and the resurrection from the dead, that Jesus has been given a name above every name. We see that all power in Heaven and earth has been given to Him. Revelation 11:15 also says,

"The kingdoms of this world became the kingdoms of our Lord and of His Christ, and He shall reign for ever and ever!"

Through the cross, Jesus has been exalted and glorified. Revelation also tells us that the kingdoms of the earth have become the Lord's. This temptation would cause Jesus to receive His promise prematurely and through compromising efforts. It was always in God's will to give Jesus the kingdoms of the world, but in order for Him to receive them, He had to go to the cross. Jesus had to defeat hell and the grave. He had to endure all the pain of the cross. The enemy propositioned Jesus with a shortcut. All Jesus had to do was to bow before Satan and he would give him the kingdoms of the earth. Jesus rebuked him and decided to press through toward the goal that was set before Him. The enemy will try to get you to forfeit your assignment by taking the easy way out. It is always better to follow God all the way, overtaking a shortcut with the devil. This season of validation is designed to prove your commitment and dedication to the call.

King David's story of becoming King is extremely fascinating. In 1 Samuel 16, we see David being anointed privately in his home by the prophet Samuel. God selected David over his brother's even though he was the last one to come into the presence of the prophet. When Samuel anointed David, he received the full measure of his anointing as a leader and a king. Although he had not been through a formal training season, he was still anointed. David's anointing did not indicate that it was his time to be king because Saul was still on the throne. We see in 1 Samuel 17, that David defeated the Philistine champion, Goliath. David exemplified the courage of a king when he was willing to stand up to Goliath on behalf of the people of Israel. The entire public action displayed his anointing and valor to the people of Israel. It showed the makings of a great warrior and king. As a result, David was invited to the kings court. In 1 Samuel 18:4-5, we see King Saul's son, Jonathan, abdicating his right to the throne and giving it to David.

1 Samuel 18 says,

And Jonathan stripped himself of the robe that was on him and gave it to David, and his armor, and even his sword and his bow and his belt. And David went out and was successful wherever Saul sent him, so that Saul set him over the men of war. And this was good in the sight of all the people and also in the sight of Saul's servants.

The action of Jonathan giving his robe to David was his way of validating that David was anointed to be the king of Israel. Jonathan essentially dressed David as that crowned prince.

Later in 1 Samuel Chapter 18, we see the beginning of a conflict between David and King Saul. When David and Saul were returning from battle, the women came out of the cities and celebrated with singing and dancing. They sang to one another chanting, "Saul has struck down his thousands, and David, ten thousand." Saul heard this and was extremely angry. The Bible details how it incited internal insecurity in the king. He said, *"They have ascribed to David ten thousands, and me they have ascribed one thousand, and what more can he have but the kingdom."* The Bible tells us that Saul began looking at David differently from that day on. It was a public decree that the people started to acknowledge David and his anointing. This caused Saul great anxiety and insecurity. The truth is, due to Saul's sin, he was essentially fired from his role as the king. David was selected to be the next king of Israel. Saul had to live with the personal conflict of losing the throne, and now he had the inward taunting of witnessing his successor grow in popularity amongst the people. This was emotionally devastating for the king of Israel. Saul's jealousy grew to the point of trying to kill David. In the season of validation, we may encounter the spirit of Saul that would try to kill or discredit us before our time to emerge. The spirit of Saul is assigned to this season to cause intimidation and assignment abandonment.

1 Samuel 22 shows David being confirmed in his leadership further. Although he is not the king, he started leading a small

army of four hundred men. They saw David's courage and submitted to his leadership. In the season of validation, people may begin to follow your leadership. The temptation is to move in this season prematurely. In the validation season, there is a level of leadership

THE SPIRIT OF SAUL IS ASSIGNED TO THIS SEASON TO CAUSE INTIMIDATION AND ASSIGNMENT ABANDONMENT.

that one must carry out, though it is not yet time to walk in the full measure of the assignment. This season is a time of cultivation for the ultimate call. In 1 Samuel 24, David was confronted with the ultimate test of maturity and restraint. David was in close enough proximity to kill Saul, but decided not to. David had to choose honor over dishonor. Saul had been vicious towards David, but God was using this situation to train David as a leader.

In 1 Samuel 30, David and his men were at war, and their enemy came and raided their camp. They took everything from them. The people were in distress and thought to stone David. However, the Bible tells us that David inquired of the Lord and the Lord gave him the insight needed to lead his people further. This was another test of trusting in the Lord in the midst of tragedy. Every negative situation was used to further develop David into the great king that he was.

EQUIPPED FOR THE VALIDATION SEASON

There are five things that we must do to be equipped to pass this season of validation. The first thing is to *watch the temptation to step out from covering before the right time.* Just because one is great at what they do does not always mean that it is the right time to launch out. I have seen this happen when people have started businesses before they were ready and it was met with devastating results. I have also seen people start ministries when they were not ready and the ministry failed. When I speak of covering, I am referring to mentorship and support. A great mentor will not limit you when it is time to grow and expand. However, it is important to understand timing and seasons.

> **THE FIRST THING IS TO WATCH THE TEMPTATION TO STEP OUT FROM COVERING BEFORE THE RIGHT TIME.**

Secondly, *To pass this season, one must be proven in their ability to lead and show maturity in their giftedness.* Just having a gift is not good enough. There must be a level of mastery in using that gift to be ready to lead. I have seen so many people talk about what they are good at doing or what they will do without seeing any real fruit from their seasons of preparation and training. Being a leader is more than just thinking you are a good leader; it takes preparation and training. As you are being developed, it is important to make sure that moments of opportunities and training are maximized to ensure that your life will produce great results. This happens when we choose to persevere through difficult times and refuse to give up because things are hard. Be careful not to quit

75

prematurely or before you can extract everything a season has to teach you.

> ## SECONDLY, *TO PASS THIS SEASON, ONE MUST BE PROVEN IN THEIR ABILITY TO LEAD AND SHOW MATURITY IN THEIR GIFTEDNESS.*

Third, *Emerging leaders must refuse the desire to kill Saul.* I don't mean literally killing Saul, but this is the temptation of disregarding, disrespecting and dishonoring leaders that have led before you. Just because we know that we are called to eventually replace someone doesn't mean that we should disrespect them. Many emerging leaders step into dishonor because they feel that the previous generation is irrelevant. The goal in this season is to fight to maintain honor. This is especially true, when the Saul spirit is trying to disparage your character and representation. It is the time to stay submitted to the Lord until it is your season. The priority is to honor the previous generation and wait on the timing of the Lord to release you into your season. Please note that, the priority is to hear and obey God. This sea-

> ## *EMERGING LEADERS MUST REFUSE THE DESIRE TO KILL SAUL.*

son is less about man and all about God. God is the one who promotes and demotes. The caution is to make sure that your process is handled delicately. This can only happen when we are completely submitted to the will of God.

Fourth, *Watch the temptation of thinking more of yourself than you should.* It is funny; I don't know any other way to say this but to say it this way! Don't allow the applause of man to cause you to get a big head. Many leaders listen to the praises of men and allow themselves to get distracted. It can happen when people begin to compliment and encourage emerging leaders regarding what they can do. The goal in all that we do is the maintain a spirit of humility. God resists the proud and gives favor to the humble. Although the emerging leader may be extremely gifted, they must remember that gift belongs to the Lord.

The last thing to remember in this season is to maintain a strong life with the Lord. The closer you get to your season of leadership requires a higher level of consecration and communion with God. Developing a strong spiritual life is key to making sure we stay close to God's heart and voice to know what the next will be. The best ways to cultivate our giftedness is in the presence of the Lord.

> **WATCH THE TEMPTATION OF THINKING MORE OF YOURSELF THAN YOU SHOULD.**

CHAPTER 6

The Assignment: EMERGE

A definition for "emerge" is to become prominent and to come into view. This chapter focuses on the season of assignment. Every season of our life prepares us for destiny. I believe that all of the warfare we encounter in our developing years is intended to derail us from the season where we come into the full purpose of why we were created. I also believe that the Lord uses every situation, experience, issue, and lesson to help shape us into who we were intended to become. One of the best scriptural examples of this is Joseph.

This chapter speaks to the person who has been processed and proven and is now prepared to walk in their calling. If this is

> **THE LORD USES EVERY SITUATION, EXPERIENCE, ISSUE, AND LESSON TO HELP SHAPE US INTO WHO WE WERE INTENDED TO BECOME.**

you, it is important that you accept the fullness of your call and pursue purpose with all that you have. This season is not to be passive regarding your assignment, but instead, it is the time to be passionate. God is saying to you, it's time for you to take your rightful place as a leader in whatever capacity you have been called to impact. As stated earlier in this book, we are in a deficit regarding leadership. It is necessary for the people of God to be cultivated to lead in different areas of society.

When I was at Oral Roberts University, the Lord really placed Romans 8:19 on my heart. I recall being almost captivated by this scripture, and it would not leave me. To be honest, I could not explain it theologically, and I would not even attempt to try. All I recall is this scripture leaving an imprint on my spirit that actually changed my understanding of the assignment. The scripture says,

"For the earnest expectation of the creation eagerly waits for the revealing of the sons of God."

Romans 8:19

I remember reading this scripture and pressing into a place of truth.

In my understanding, I believed this scripture spoke of the earth waiting for the sons of God to manifest or come forth. I believe in every generation; we see various aspects of wickedness. We know that the world has been subjected to corruption, being that the enemy is the prince and the power of the air. In this, the world is in chaos. There are many systems and aspects of our world that are bound under the powers of darkness. The Bible says that we wrestle not against flesh and blood but principalities and rulers of darkness. The earth is being controlled by evil powers, and they aim to oppress people from discovering the truth of Christ. These powers set out to cause people to live under wicked leaders, nations, and laws.

These principalities represent the rulers that create corrupt governments. The devastation we see with people (Example: poverty, violence, social unrest, and drugs) is a byproduct of an overall problem. This problem is simple, the enemy. The earth is eagerly waiting for God's children to emerge to take their rightful place. I believe the answers and solutions to the world's problems are in the body of Christ. The church has been left on the earth with the intention to be a resource. All creation is waiting for the children of God to emerge and bring deliverance and freedom.

This scripture helped to change my paradigm regarding the church of the Lord Jesus Christ. I love the church, and I am a true definition of a church boy. I have been in the church all my life, and it has shaped and molded me into the man I am today. This scripture began, in me, the development of a greater understanding of the church. In Matthew 16, Jesus asks His disciples who did people say that He was. His disciplines responded by telling Jesus who the people said he was. He followed up this question with an even more profound question; He directly asked His disciples, but who do you say that I am. Peter responds and says, "You are the Christ the Son of the living God." Jesus responds to this and says to Peter that upon the revelation of Jesus (The Rock), He would build His church, and the gates of hell will not prevail against it. Jesus has established the church in the earth to stand in the midst of the wickedness of the world and take authority over it through His name. The body of Christ has the responsibility to tear down the works of Satan and reestablish works that reflect the plan of God in the earth.

This concept was new to me in my ORU (Oral Roberts University) days, I was a church kid and I wanted to have church. My vision for life and success was to do something in the church and be "full-time" doing it. I loved church and just wanted to have church. I wanted to sing in the choir, go to church services and revivals, shout and listen to good preaching. I had an extremely polarizing perspective of the church and the world. I could never imagine someone being "called" to the world. I definitely did not understand how one could actually impact the world. God used Romans 8:19 to open my eyes to the fact that there is a need in the world for God's children to emerge.

The church is made up of people. Every believer has a space in the earth that they have been called to influence and occupy. As members of the church, we have been given the right to access Heaven and bring Heaven down to earth. It is the collective call of the church. God places local churches in cities, regions, and areas to prevail against the darkness. The local church and the universal church are called to have influence. This influence happens when the members understand their individual call. The days of just being a pew member of a church has to stop. We are in a season where the Lord is inspiring people to understand as a member of the family of God, they have a right to claim territory and to take it. This call is not only for pastors, this is a call to every son and daughter of God.

LESSONS FROM JOSEPH.

After two whole years, Pharaoh dreamed that he was standing by the Nile, and behold, there came up out of the Nile seven cows, attractive and plump, and they fed in the reed grass. And behold, seven other cows, ugly and thin, came up out of the Nile after them, and stood by the other cows on the bank of the Nile. And the ugly, thin cows ate up the seven attractive, plump cows. And Pharaoh awoke. And he fell asleep and dreamed a second time. And behold, seven ears of grain, plump and good, were growing on one stalk. And behold, after them sprouted seven ears, thin and blighted by the east wind. And the thin ears swallowed up the seven plump, full ears. And Pharaoh awoke, and behold, it was a dream. So in the morning his spirit was troubled, and he sent and called for all the magicians of Egypt and all its wise men. Pharaoh told them his dreams, but there was none who could interpret them to Pharaoh. Then the chief cupbearer said to Pharaoh, "I remember my offenses today. When Pharaoh was angry with his servants and put me and the chief baker in custody in the house of the captain of the guard, we dreamed on the same night, he and I, each having a dream with its own interpretation. A young Hebrew was there with us, a servant of the captain of the guard. When we told him, he interpreted our dreams to us, giving an interpretation to each man according to his dream. And as he interpreted to us, so it came about. I was restored to my office, and the baker was hanged." Then Pharaoh sent and called Joseph, and they quickly brought him out of the pit. And when he had shaved himself and changed his clothes, he came in before Pharaoh.

Genesis 41:1-12 ESV

We need leaders to take their seats. I believe we have entered a moment in time where God is making specific ways for His people to come forth in their assignment and calling. In this scripture, we are witnessing Joseph getting ready to emerge into his life assignment and his season to occupy a seat of influence in the land of Egypt.

We are first introduced to Joseph in Genesis 37. We know him as the favored son of Jacob. Joseph was born to Jacob in his old age. Jacob's love for Joseph was demonstrated by him giving his son a robe of many colors. This robe essentially represented his position or mantle in his family. Joseph possessed abilities of management and leadership at a youthful age. In Genesis 37, we see that Joseph was the manager of his father's house and he was given the responsibility on checking on them as they did their work, Joseph also possessed a special gift of dreams and had a prophetic call. Joseph dreamed a dream of his destiny that his brothers would essentially bow down to him, and he would rise up as a leader in his father's house and the land.

Joseph was hated by his brothers. First, he talked too much! Just because he had a dream did not mean that he had to run and tell his family. There are some things that God reveals to us that we should keep to ourselves. We see this with Mary when the angel came to her about Jesus. The Bible says that she pondered what was said in her heart. Sometimes our loved ones cannot comprehend what God is saying regarding our assignment and it may be best that God reveals His plans to people by the grace on our life, and not through what we say. Secondly, he was hated by his brothers because his father favored him. Jacob knew that there was something special about Joseph and loved him deeply. Thirdly, Joseph's giftedness and talents were extraordinary. His father placed the management of all his sons on Joseph. He was brilliant and had excellent integrity. His character and gifts differentiated Joseph from his brothers. They even labeled him "that dreamer," out of frustration of who he was and what he was seeing. They used his giftedness and call to bring a wedge between them. Ultimately this hatred led Joseph's brothers to sell him eventually.

I wonder how Joseph reconciled the fact that he was hated by his brothers so much that they considered killing him and then eventually selling him into slavery. Many times, our natural gifts can cause people to develop envy towards us. This mainly happens to leaders with extraordinary giftedness. You may recall the times where you felt as if you were disregarded and mistreated because of your call. Developing leaders often feel misplaced and misunderstood. It happens as a result of people trying to box leaders in. As a leader, you can't be boxed in! True leaders operate at a higher frequency of vision and many people are not able to keep up. If you feel that you have been overlooked and disregarded, please be encouraged to know that you are being cultivated for a season of leadership that is greater than where you are now.

Joseph spent years in a season of exile. God showed Joseph a vision of who he would emerge to become, but God did not tell Joseph everything that would transpire in his process of development. I have found this to be the case repeatedly. God always reveals the end and seems to leave out the in-between details. The vision revealed assists us in staying in faith as we process through the season of development. Genesis 39 tells us that Joseph was sold into slavery and purchased by Potiphar, the captain of Pharaoh's guard. Potiphar was a just man and showed Joseph great favor. Imagine this, he was favored by his father, and now he is being favored by his master. This favor was due to his brilliance, giftedness, and management ability. Joseph was on his way to the seat of leadership that he saw in his dream, but went on a serious journey in getting there. Potiphar's house was an essential stop on the way to his assignment.

Potiphar's house represented Joseph's apprenticeship season. Although a slave, Joseph maintained great character and integrity during this season. We must understand that every season and life experience we are privileged to endure is a part of our perfecting process. The key is to maintain the proper perspective recognizing that God is faithful and His promises are always sure and true. Joseph's gifts became more refined in Potiphar's house and his responsibilities were even greater than his responsibilities with his father. Joseph was now managing all the offers of the house, and was running the business of the household. In every season of process, God increases our capacity. This was an opportunity for Joseph to learn how to

> **WE MUST UNDERSTAND THAT EVERY SEASON AND LIFE EXPERIENCE WE ARE PRIVILEGED TO ENDURE IS A PART OF OUR PERFECTING PROCESS.**

lead and steward what belonged to another. It is important to recognize that although Joseph had great favor and influence, it was not his landing place in reference to the assignment.

While he was successfully leading this household, he met an evil spirit purposed to discredit him. This spirit desired to get Joseph off course and derail him through lust. Potiphar's wife grew an attraction for Joseph and began enticing him. It is easy to look at this situation from one level of simple lust, but it is important to dig deeper to understand what was precisely at work here. Joseph had the responsibility of stewarding everything in Potiphar's house. He was able to act as the leader of the house in the place of Potiphar, but he was not the leader. This woman was the wife of Joseph's master and she was off-limits to Joseph. This house was not Joseph's house. The enticement was more than a sexual temptation, it was a temptation of power, ego, and covetousness. We must be careful to represent our place and not fall prey to the temptation to covet what belongs to another. This situation was a test. The temptation was intended to cause Joseph to fail, by taking what was not intended to be his. You can steward a man's work, but that does not mean that work belongs to you.

When I was 21, as I previously mentioned, I served as an assistant to a pastor. One time during my service to this church, the pastor grew ill. It was my role to oversee the ministries while my pastor was out. I was given the responsibility of oversight, but I was not the senior pastor. My decisions had to keep in line with the vision and directives of the senior leader. Anything otherwise would have been dishonoring. I have witnessed people time and time again fail this test. Just because you have favor in a company or ministry doesn't mean that you are ready to lead it. Joseph was favored, but his favor had limits. Thank God Joseph passed this test and temptation. Joseph denied this woman and it led to

Potiphar's wife accusing him of attempted rape. As a result of this accusation, Joseph was placed in prison with prisoners of the king.

Imagine being a slave in a foreign land and now being a prisoner, depressing, right? Think of Joseph's possible inward turmoil and warfare. Consider his emotional well-being as he lived in prison. Joseph goes from being his daddy's favored son, to being the favored slave and now a prisoner. Joseph must have felt forsaken by God. History tells us that Joseph spent ten years in this prison. Up until this point, Joseph had not done anything wrong; all he did was to be a man called by God to save a nation.

God's mind is so expansive and many times it is way too complicated to understand. As a leader, I will never understand why God does what He does with people. I would never understand why He seems always to take His people through the wilderness. I have never heard a story of a leader that was easy or simple. There are so many stories of people who were told many no's before they got one yes that changed their life. People talk about all of the pain and misery that they endured before they experienced success. Joseph, too, experienced the workings of God. He placed Joseph in that prison until the right moment that his gift was needed.

The Bible says in Isaiah 55:8,
"For my thoughts are not your thoughts, neither are your ways my ways, declares the Lord."

Sometimes we go through things and don't understand why, but the situation is the providence of the Lord. The main objective is to trust the Lord in the process.

KEEPING THE FAITH

Jude 1:3 says,

> *"Beloved, while I was very diligent to write to you concerning our common salvation, I found it necessary to write to you exhorting you to contend earnestly for the faith which was once for all delivered to the saints."*

This scripture tells us that we must *contend* for the faith that was once delivered to the saints. The word *contend* speaks of fighting for or struggling with. We have been called to fight with tenacity for the faith that was delivered to the saints. It is the faith that the early church had to endure persecution and scrutiny for the gospel. There is a real warfare that comes against people when they are being prepared to emerge. The enemy tries his best to distract and cause us to not walk in destiny. The warfare is to stay in the truth of the word and what the Lord has spoken. The concepts regarding purpose are revealed in this season are intended to ground you for the journey ahead. It is why the prophetic word spoken is a needful and powerful tool. True prophetic words are intended to build faith and hope towards what is to come. If the word is from God, we have the ability to contend for that word through prayer, fasting, study worship, and education. The Lord uses many different ways to speak to his people so that they can be certain of His voice. Joseph had two prophetic dreams before he went through the season of exile. I personally believe that the clarity of the words to Joseph through his dreams helped to keep him during his time of devastation. Let me decree to you that you are just passing through this season and you will not be here forever. The Lord is about to blow your mind with what he does next in your life.

> ## YOU ARE JUST PASSING THROUGH THIS SEASON AND YOU WILL NOT BE HERE FOREVER.

IT'S TIME TO EMERGE

Joseph's life chronicles the process of development and preparation of a leader. While Joseph was in prison, the king had a dream he did not understand. Scripture tells us that no one in the entire country could interpret the meaning of the king's dream. While Joseph was in prison, he accurately interpreted the dreams of two of the king's servants. In the king's distress, his servant who was previously imprisoned with Joseph, remembered Joseph's incredible ability of interpreting dreams and announced to Pharaoh there was a young foreigner in prison who could interpret this dream. Joseph maintained his integrity and served well in the prison. Although this time was long, God was setting Joseph up to walk in his assignment. This prison was just a holding place. It was essentially the perfect place for him to meet the right people to get to his destiny. As I stated earlier, God's mind is expansive and we will never be able to understand why He does what He does. One thing that is sure is that God is good and He has good plans for us. Once the king heard of this young Hebrew who could interpret dreams, he sent for Joseph. Please remember this, when it is your season to walk into destiny, nothing can hinder you. The king did not worry about him being a foreign fugitive.

Joseph is from a small clan of people in comparison to the nation of Egypt. He was a major gift and his potential was bigger than his family's influence. For the world to experience the fullness of his giftedness, he needed to be connected to a stronger nation. All while Joseph was serving his father and serving Potiphar, God was cultivating a national leader. God was preparing him for his season to emerge. When the king heard of Joseph's ability, the Bible says that he sent for Joseph. The king did not care about his past. The king did care about his history. The king had a need and that was all that mattered. Joseph could address the king's need.

Genesis 41: 14 says,
Then Pharaoh sent and called Joseph, and they brought him quickly out of the dungeon; and he shaved, changed his clothing, and came to Pharaoh.

Joseph had spent years in bondage and in prison, when it was his time to emerge, the Bible says that the king sent for him and quickly brought him out of the pit. I love this verse that points out how Joseph shaved and changed his clothes. Joseph shaved off the despair of the past and the old season, and got himself prepared for his next. He was getting ready to walk in his season of destiny. As you are getting ready to walk in your assignment, make sure you let the past be the past and take the right steps to move into your future. You can't walk into the palace, looking like a prisoner. It is time to cast off your old man, and embrace the person you have been called to become.

> **MAKE SURE YOU LET THE PAST BE THE PAST AND TAKE THE RIGHT STEPS TO MOVE INTO YOUR FUTURE.**

The world's systems are failing and are messing up. The kings in the earth need the insight that has been deposited into the children of God. I believe we are in the Joseph generation, where God is releasing particular gifts and callings upon his people to bring transformation to our world. God desires for us to be available for these opportunities. This can only happen when we submit to His will and allow ourselves to be processed. Imagine if Joseph had allowed himself to be overtaken by depression when he was in the pit. Or if he would have stopped being a leader after being sentenced to prison. What if he had been bitter to his family and shut down altogether? If he had failed in his seasons of processing, he would not have been ready to take on his assignment well.

The "emerge" season is the season of destiny. It is the time that all your life experiences come together and you find yourself being prepared to do your assignment in ways that you didn't know. The Lord has ordered your steps and every experience that you have had up until this point has been preparing you for your season of assignment. The key to being successful in this season is gaining the skills in every season that has led you to this point. Every season of preparation is not always wonderful, and there may be scares along the way. We must learn to take the good and the bad and use all of it for the glory of God. Joseph got the call from the king and he shaved and changed his clothes. He refused to meet his destiny with the clothes of his past season still on. He took off the clothes of his struggle and prepared himself for the next. You cannot go into your new season with old hang-ups. This is why it is important that you deal with the issues of your past. Too many times people go through life without processing all of the hurt that life has caused. We must heal and allow ourselves to be strengthened through every experience.

Destiny is not an event. Joseph's assignment was not just to interpret Pharaoh's dream, his assignment was to govern the kingdom. God used this one opportunity to position him for destiny. Joseph was always destined for greatness. This was the dream that he had when he was young. The emergence season is the time that God brings your dreams to pass and gives you the full understanding of why you went through what you went through. Joseph had work to do and his past was all preparation. Joseph walked through this door and never looked back. One part of his assignment was to preserve the lineage of Jesus that was promised to his ancestors. Joseph had to be a leader in a superpower nation to protect his family from the great famine. His father's house did not have the influence or resources to aid his leadership in preserving a generation. The Lord intentionally placed him in Egypt because Egypt had the resource to accompany his greatness. Joseph was rejected by his family, but this was the best things that could have ever happened to him. If he had been accepted, he would have never been sent to Egypt. Rejection is not a bad thing; it is just a sign that a space, season, company, situation, or group of people do not have the capacity for what you carry.

The Lord has placed something significant in you and the earth is in desperate need for your gift's full expression to be revealed. Once the season opens up for you to walk into destiny, there should be a continual process of development. Because God is eternal, our callings are from eternity, our ability to grow, and be further cultivated in our potential is limitless. Truthfully, we place limits on what we do and who we can become. When God opens the door for destiny, it is our responsibility to maximize the season. When it is your time do all that you can do, make sure you pour out as much as you can. I have intentionally used the language of "season" throughout this book. The emerge season or the assignment season is not forever. This season comes at a particular time when your gift is the most useful for your lifetime. This season is not always connected to age, but our age and stage in life can often have a lot to do with how we move in this space of life.

There are certain things that you can only do when you are younger and there are somethings that you can only do when you are more mature. Take an athlete for an example. All their lives, they train for their season to be a professional. Athletes have a specific time when their body is at its peak. As we see, when athletes age, their stamina decreases, and their ability to perform in the same manner of their youth diminishes. Their season then must change to something else. This shifting does not mean to leave the sport, but it can mean to take on a different capacity. This may look like coaching, training, commentating, or even on the business side of things. When you are in the season of assignment it is important to maximize your season. Do all that you can do and all that God has placed in your heart in this season.

Our assignments are all connected to the greatest assignment given to the church, the great commission. We have been given the responsibility to go into all the world and make disciples. Our calling is connected to the promotion of the gospel of Jesus Christ. As you step into your season of leadership, remember your call is higher and greater than you. It is in this commission that each of us have been called into leadership. This great commission was not given to a select group of people. This commission was given to all disciples. All believers are leaders and have the capacity to lead.

One of the great failures of our day is not training every person to accept their call into leadership. Everyone has the capacity to lead and should be cultivated to accept the areas they have been called to steward. In leadership, there are various leadership levels. Everyone is not called to be a CEO, but every person who works for the company should see themselves bringing their leadership to the corporation. Every space in the world has a place for the people of God to step in and show their brilliance and transformational ability. I believe the deficit in leadership we see is due to people not being connected to a sense of personal assignment and calling. Our educational system is not designed to assist people in discovering their unique brilliance. Our educational systems are designed for people to work a job. We have people who seek careers based on their passions, but people often have to discover passion outside of formal educational frameworks. I believe this issue is because our traditional education model is based on reading, writing, and arithmetic.

These areas are important, but the greatest need is the cultivation of giftedness. If a person is never placed in a position to discover their gifts, they will never feel confident to lead. Understanding individual giftedness is the gateway to a purposeful life. Our assignments are connected to our giftedness. Our passions are typically connected to our giftedness. Our destinies are actualized through our giftedness. We emerge to a place of prominence through the cultivation of our gifts. God put Joseph through various seasons of development to perfect him for his destiny. By the time Joseph stood in front of Pharoah, he was a master of his ability to interpret the king's dream with ease and give him counsel with confidence. Pharoah did not meet the young man who talked too much. He met the young man skilled to lead a nation.   The Lord is going to grant you access when you are ready. You will know your readiness through honest assessment. Once you have passed every test and have been proven, you are ready to occupy. It is time for you to emerge!

CHAPTER 7

The Legacy Season

It is December 2009, and fans are excited for the return of a superstar. Whitney Houston was embarking on her come back tour to support what would be her final album, *"I Look To You."* The album had been received well, and people were excited to see her live and in concert. Whitney had done some major TV appearances and had seemed to have had great feedback regarding her album. Critics and fans had celebrated the triumph of her return but noted that her voice was different. It is no secret that Whitney Houston's voice had declined significantly due to her lifestyle. The tour was met with positive expectations, however, it ended up with disappointed fans, unfavorable tabloid stories, and negative reports of her performances. Whitney, who had been known as one of the greatest singers of all time, was now considered a vocal failure. Whitney had lost her incredible voice and had been deemed as a "has been." She is one of the best-selling artists of all time and is also one of the most awarded singers, but her later years would forever be embedded in people's hearts as a failure. The sad reality is that although she was brilliant in her craft and loved by so many, her life did not end well. We can celebrate her accomplishments and undeniable talent, but one could argue that her life failures overshadows her success. Her legacy is one of drug abuse, a tumultuous relationship, a failed comeback, and a tragic death.

Whitney's story is too similar to so many other artists whose lives ended in extreme tragedy. There are stories of many leaders who have done great work, but are remembered by scandal and significant failure due to their character flaws and lack of integrity. It is necessary to understand that how we end a thing is just as important to how we began it. Destiny is not an event but a time where one is allowed to walk in the fullness of their earth assignment. The emerge season is when God allows us to come into purpose, but this season can be temporary if our time is not stewarded well. Many young people think that they will always be young, but we know that this is not the case. The emerge season is the entry point into destiny, but this season is to be managed intentionally.

Time is precious, and you can never recover lost time. Every day that we live, we are one day closer to the day that we will die. This reality should place the greatest burden on us to be intentional with our time. Authentic leaders understand that they are not here forever and they create organizations and systems that can function well beyond their years. This happens when leaders are committed to building a legacy. Legacy is people's remembrance of us once we are no longer alive. Essentially legacy speaks of spiritual and natural inheritance. True leaders build with the end in mind.

> **AUTHENTIC LEADERS UNDERSTAND THAT THEY ARE NOT HERE FOREVER AND THEY CREATE ORGANIZATIONS AND SYSTEMS THAT CAN FUNCTION WELL BEYOND THEIR YEARS,**

I have been blessed with great mentors, leaders, and pastors. My pastor, Dr. Fred L. Hodge, Jr., is the senior pastor of Living Praise Christian Church in the Los Angeles area. His voice and leadership have been vital to my development and ministry. Early on in our relationship, I recall a meeting that we had. This meeting was essentially an official discussion about my vision for ministry and he was providing me pastoral counsel. After I had shared my vision for ministry, he asked me a question that really changed my perspective on what I was building. Dr. Hodge asked, "When you get to the end of your life, what do you want to have accomplished?" He said that knowing the end was important to assist me as I began my journey. His question impacted me greatly. This meeting took place at an interesting point in my life. I was working at a job that I hated, considering church planting and a newlywed. Indeed I was not in my season of leadership; I was an emerging leader with vision, zeal, and passion. My vision was connected at the time with all the things I wanted to do in the future. As I reflect on my former self, I am certain that I told him a lot of different ideas without having a structured perspective and vision. I was still at the place where I was trying my best to articulate what I was thinking and not confident in what I was doing. His question and, later advice, gave me great perspective. I am in a different place of life now and I am intentionally building what I want to see at the end of my life.

It is easy to get lost in all of the excitement that is associated when we start to see our dreams come true and we begin to emerge. It is fun to finally get a seat at the table, when that has been something that we have always wanted. It is an amazing thing how God is able to take a person out of obscurity and bring them into a place of prominence seemingly overnight. It's especially true in the era we live in now. It seems as if all we need is one viral video or social media post and our life can change instantly. So many times, people invest their life into something and when they finally get it, they don't really know what to do. Once they get what they have desired the the vision should be to sustain it. It is tough, when things are happening for us at a fast pace. The temptation is to grow and do as much as possible, but this is not the most strategic thing to do. The proper strategy uses the momentum and possible resources of the moment to build sustainable systems and strong teams. This requires work and greater discipline. We have often heard it said that our gifts open the doors, but it is our character that keeps us there. As we build, we must make sure that our character is a priority. Our character and integrity become the nuts and bolts of our brand and legacy. Doing great acts and having great wins mean nothing when character and integrity are lacking. When one's character is faulty, people will celebrate their accomplishments for a season, but will eventually discredit them because of the damage they have caused.

> OUR CHARACTER AND
> INTEGRITY BECOME THE
> NUTS AND BOLTS OF OUR
> BRAND AND LEGACY.

The Bible is clear that we must not place our treasures on these of the earth.

Matthew 6:19-21 says,

"Do not lay up for yourselves treasures on earth, where moth and rust destroy and where thieves break in and steal; but lay up for yourselves treasures in heaven, where neither moth nor rust destroys and where thieves do not break in and steal. For where your treasure is, there your heart will be also."

When we build to be big, or to just be famous, we are placing our treasure on things of the earth. Yes, we should reach as many people as possible, but the priority of what we are doing should never be focused on temporal things. Our callings are Heaven ordained and they have a connection to a greater purpose. All God-given callings are released in the earth for the purpose of bringing the people of that generation closer to God. The assignment on your life has nothing to do with you and everything to do with God. Investing our treasure to build a personal empire is carnal. Our investment should always be in making God more known on the earth.

Once we have emerged in our leadership and have invested the right effort and energy into our assignment, we are prepared to transition into the legacy season well. When a person is in the legacy phase of their life, they are not worried about building and expanding. Many times this season is a more relaxed season than the past ones. This season is more about sustaining, depositing, and investing in what has been built to make sure it is able to stand the test of time. When a leader is in their legacy phase, they should not be concerned with all the details of the operation, by this time, everything should be intact. The leader should be able to take an objective perspective and provide course correction when necessary. In this season, a leader is actively searching or has passed the mantle of leadership to another so that they can be a coach. This season does not speak of ultimate retirement, but moving one's efforts in ministry to imparting wisdom and mentorship.

> **THIS SEASON DOES NOT SPEAK OF ULTIMATE RETIREMENT, BUT MOVING ONE'S EFFORTS IN MINISTRY TO IMPARTING WISDOM AND MENTORSHIP.**

MOMENTUM IS THE KEY

One of my favorite sports is track and field. Honestly, I love everything about the sport and the athleticism that it takes to train and compete. I grew up running track with my family and I have learned so much about life from years as a track runner. I am still a runner and I often think of my training when I run. My favorite event is the 4 x 1 relay. To know track and field, you know that it is essentially an individual sport. Track runners race other athletes, but the goal is to always perfect one's personal time. A person can be a star runner on a bad team and still be celebrated for their achievements. The relay is the only event that requires a team effort. The development and the technical aspects of putting a relay team together are also interesting. I have seen relays where they place the fastest runner at the end or at the second leg. I have seen some relays that have been put together with runners who weren't as fast on the straights, but strong on the curves, so they made the 3rd or first legs of the relay. When I used to run, we would spend a lot of time practicing passing the baton. The key to this was learning the team's rhythm and to run fast enough to match the teammate's speed as they are passing the baton to you. The key to the relay is to keep the momentum and not to drop the baton.

IT IS GOD'S DESIRE FOR MINISTRY AND ASSIGNMENTS TO CONTINUE ON THE EARTH.

Years ago, in prayer, the Lord showed me a relay and explained to me that it is important to keep the momentum of ministry with the generations that have preceded me. He told me that this only happened when the baton is passed correctly. It is God's desire for ministry and assignments to continue on the earth. It is not His intention for works to end once the leader transitions out of that role. It's a big issue that I see generationally. Many leaders struggle with their transition process. So many thriving ministries and businesses decline because a leader doesn't properly assess their season. Other ministries fail because they do not keep up with the momentum of the move. Learning when and how to transition takes wisdom and maturity. To do this well, the leader must see the organization as a bigger entity than themselves. A leader must also hold the health of the organization to the highest priority. This happens when leaders are not insecure and can be honest about their effectiveness. A leader should never be a hindrance to the progression of a work.

If the work is God designed and inspired, it means the assignment of what has been built is greater than the person assigned to the task of building or leading it. The Lord wants to make sure that His vision is actualized in the earth and that it maintains its potency. It is a tragedy to see businesses and ministries that have experienced great success in the past decline. Many leaders attribute the decline to some type of spiritual attack, when simply it just needs a shifting in reference to the leadership structure. It sometimes may not be the devil at all, but a stubborn leader who refuses to invest in a successor and move into a different assignment. In order to secure one's legacy, the baton has to be passed.

DROPPED MANTLES AND DROPPED ASSIGNMENTS

Earlier in this book, I covered the story of Elisha and Elijah. This story is a common story that presents relevant truth regarding leadership and ministry. In 2 Kings 2, we see the story of Elijah being caught up in a chariot of fire and his servant, Elisha, catching his mantle. Prophet Elijah trained Elisha for six years. On the day that he would be caught up, Elisha asked Elijah for a double portion of his anointing. Elijah responded to Elisha that his request was difficult and that he would only receive it if he saw him taken up. The Bible tells us that when Elijah was taken up that his mantle fell from him to the ground. Elisha was there when this happened, and he picked up the mantle.

The mantle represented Elijah's ministry and anointing. Elijah did supernatural signs and wonders in Israel. He is known as the "prophet of fire" who, called the nation back to a place of repentance. He was an exceptional ministry gift. Just because Elijah left the earth did not mean that there was no need for his ministry to continue on the earth. He instructed Elisha to be in the right place at the right time to catch the mantle. Just because God had plans for Elijah to be taken up did not mean that the need for his ministry ended. Elijah's time had passed, but it was Elisha's time. We see in scripture that Elisha walked in a double portion of Elijah. Elisha's continuation of moving in Elijah's ministry made sure that the earth did not lose what God placed in Elijah. A different generation was blessed by the ministry and the mantle was not dropped.

I have often heard many people talk about the posture and position of Elisha in the story. It is easy to view the scripture and see that Elisha was blessed because he was in a position to be blessed. However, I think a major concept to consider is that Elijah made sure that he had someone in place to receive his mantle. Elijah invested six years of his life pouring into his

Emerge

successor. The legacy season is all about investing one's resources well into the next generation to make sure that vision continues once they arc gone.

Everyone has a mantle, and every God-inspired organization has a call. Elijah's ministry was significant, and it would have been a shame for his ministry to end because God had called him. Elijah's mantle represented his assignment to the earth. One thing to point out is that this mantle did not go with Elijah to Heaven. His mantle fell to the ground. Everything that we do in the earth for the Lord is for the advancement of the kingdom of God in the earth. When we die, we receive heavenly rewards, but we don't carry our positions or accolades to Heaven. The legacy of what we do while we are on the earth is for the people that we leave behind. The truth of the matter is that we should leave such a legacy that we continue to advance the Kingdom of Heaven even after we die. Elijah's special anointing was for his generation. We see that Elisha picked up the mantle and continued the ministry of Elijah. To be honest, Elisha continued the ministry of God. What we invest in building, should have nothing to do with us, our ego, but all about the mission behind it. When leaders build with this perspective, it is easy to build things that last beyond them. The goal is to leave when the season is over and know that your work will continue so people can be blessed way beyond your time—it is legacy.

Elijah had the hard task of training his successor. This had to take maturity and intentionality. No one wants to be replaced, and no wants to feel irrelevant. I am not saying that Elijah had these feelings, but I wonder what went through his mind when God told him to anoint Elisha to succeed him. I imagine him struggling with this reality. The scriptures do not tell us that he anointed Elisha, the Bible tells us that he threw his mantle on him and that Elisha followed him. Regardless of the details, Elijah was instructed to train the one that would take his place. I have seen organizations rise and fall based on this fact. I have unfortunately seen ministries decline because the leadership never selected and trained the next leader. I have seen organizations thrive because the leadership selected and trained the successor.

FINISHING WELL

The priority for all leaders is to finish well. In order to finish well there has to be a level of intentionality. In order to understand how one finishes well, we must look at how one finishes poorly. The Bible gives us a number of great examples of leaders who did amazing things but did not finish their assignment well. In my opinion, King Solomon's ending is probably one of the saddest in the scripture. Solomon is known as one of the greatest and wisest men that have ever lived. The Bible tells us how Solomon asked God for wisdom and how the Lord blessed him with wisdom and great wealth. We know Solomon built the first temple in Israel and that it was glorious. The Bible details Solomon's great leadership in the nation of Israel, but his life did not end well. Solomon defied God's commandments by marrying foreign women who turned his heart to other gods. The sad aspect to Solomon is the legacy that followed him, his sons did not follow after God but led the nation to greater wickedness. Solomon's life shows us that we can be great in a season, but if we make bad choices in our leadership, our legacy can be impacted.

I am in no way trying to produce fear in anyone that reads this book. We know that God has not given us a spirit of fear, but of power, love and a sound mind. Instead I intend to encourage intentionality. We must walk and lead from a place where we consider the ending of our story or assignment. Solomon had wonderful years of leadership; the problem is that his last years impacted his legacy. As leaders, we will make mistakes. However, through the mistakes, the priority is to make sure we keep our hearts close to God. His father, David, was not a perfect man, and he was not a perfect leader; however we know that he was a man after God's heart. David was willing to right his wrongs and get things right with the Lord. The way that we finish well is by constantly going back to the One who called and appointed us. When we keep Jesus at the center of all we do, we can't help but finish strong. He would not allow it any other way.

THE POWER OF IMPARTATION

For an emerging leader to receive, there must be a seasoned leader ready to impart. Impartation is a major tool that the Lord has given the body of Christ in ensuring succession and momentum.

Paul says in Romans 1:11,
For I long to see you, that I may impart to you some spiritual gift, so that you may be established—

Paul understood the power of impartation. It happens when a seasoned leader shares resources, wisdom, spends time, trains, and teaches their disciples and mentees. When Paul spent time with a church in a region, his main objective was to impart and strengthen that church for their assignment. Paul taught, corrected and freely shared what God had revealed to him. I have heard it said that some leaders struggle because they feel that up and coming leaders are not positioning themselves to receive an impartation. I have seen this and it can be a sad reality. However, one reality to consider is that some senior leaders are not positioning themselves to impart and pour because they are missing the season. It is difficult for a father to pour into sons if they are in competition. It is difficult for a leader to pour into their successor when they are still building for a ministry that reflects their particular call. Seasoned leaders must be intentional about creating spaces where they can pour into the next generation.

In 2 Timothy 1:6-7, we see the Apostle Paul encouraging his spiritual son and mentee Timothy in the Lord.

He says,

> *"Therefore I remind you to stir up the gift of God which is in you through the laying on of my hands. For God has not given us a spirit of fear, but of power and of love and of a sound mind."*

He says to him stir up the gift of God he received through the laying on of Paul's hands. Paul had spent time with Timothy and imparted into him. Paul reminds him that he received a gift from

God through the laying on of his hands. The anointing can be transferred through this practice. My favorite aspect of this verse is that Paul, the mentor, was able to tell Timothy, the mentee, to remember what he received through their time together. Paul knew what Timothy had in him, but Paul was responsible for what he received through impartation. It takes a mature leader to know what they possess and freely impart it to others.

When a leader is in their legacy season they should make it a priority to pour into as many people who are willing to receive. Pouring into others is a way of securing one's life's work. Another example of this, in scripture, is Moses and Joshua. We are introduced to Moses in the book of Exodus. Moses was born during a time where the descendants of Abraham were experiencing oppression living in Egypt. Moses grew up in Pharaoh's house, but fled after killing an Egyptian for their harsh treatment of a fellow Hebrew.

Moses encountered God through a theophany when he saw a bush that was on fire but not burned. God spoke to Moses and called him to deliver the children of Israel from the Egyptians. Moses did not grow up with the training to be a leader. Essentially, we see Moses getting a lot of on-the-job training. Moses' anointing was to build what had not been built before. God used Moses to establish the people of Israel as a nation. He developed their laws, formal religion, customs, place of worship, leadership structure, war tactics, and everything else you can imagine. Moses was a trustworthy builder. In many ways, Moses can represent a person who is called to start something great. Moses represents the innovator who starts a cutting-edge company, or the excited young church planter starting a new church. He can represent a person with fresh ideas and a new way of doing things. Moses served the people of Israel for years building a nation of people who would be the people of God. I imagine Moses experienced a lot of stress having to consistently build what had not been created. I imagine the mental agony that he felt having to deal with people who did not know what it meant to be free because they were born in bondage. Moses' life had to be difficult.

Joshua served Moses faithfully for 40 years. The Bible says in Exodus 33:11, that Joshua would not leave his master's tent. Joshua would grow to become Moses' successor in leadership of the people of Israel. The transition from Moses to Joshua as the leader of the nation of Israel was easy because Joshua had received Moses' impartation. Moses allowed his successor close and poured into him. Although Moses was not perfect and his disobedience did not allow him to walk into the promised land, his legacy was secure through Joshua and his leadership. His investment into Joshua and Joshua's submission to Moses caused the mantle to not be dropped in the nation. The people of Israel were delivered from bondage into freedom because of this impartation.

RECOGNIZING THE NEED FOR A CHANGE

One of the most significant failures a leader can make is not knowing when to transition out. Transitioning is not connected to age. Yes, age can have a role in the transition, but it is so much more than that. People can be considered young, but they have to leave what they are doing because there is a different space that requires their giftedness. A leader should never be in the way of progress for the organization. They can stunt its growth when they cannot understand the needed changes and stand in the way of the momentum. Sometimes we can only take what we build so far until we have to give it to someone else. Remember that the health of the organization should always be our priority. If we are in the way, we must make way for another.

> **ONE OF THE MOST SIGNIFICANT FAILURES A LEADER CAN MAKE IS NOT KNOWING WHEN TO TRANSITION OUT.**

There are typically signs that it is time to transition:

- The lack of passion
- The climate of the team
- Loss of interest
- Lack of relevance and influence
- Fatigue
- Physical issues

The lack of passion is a major indicator that there is time for a change. We should never lead out of duty; we should lead out of a sense of passion and purpose. When we begin to lose passion, it is time to give up the assignment. People can stay in a role because it provides them levels of security. They decide to not transition because they are nervous to what will happen to them in the next season. If the passion and joy are gone, it is time to consider what the Lord would have you to do next. We often can feel this, and we can see it in our productivity. A leader with no passion can lead the organization into disaster.

Another sign that indicates a need for a leader to shift is the climate of the team. Often the morale of the staff and team can be a sign that we may need to change. Typically, the staff takes on the leader's disposition and if the leader is not well-liked or respected, the staff will exemplify this in the culture. When there are consistent staff issues, it is necessary to take some deep introspective looks at the leader's contribution to the culture. Sometimes leaders can lose their influence and do not possess the same level of respect. It can be for a number of different reasons. It can be due to poor decisions made by the leader, or a leader that is out of touch. It can even happen when the leader loses passion, and then hinders that passion of their team by their disposition and attitude. When this happens, it may be a time to consider transitioning or doing some serious changes to fix the culture.

Losing interest in what you are doing can be considered a form of losing passion, but I think it is something greater. When a leader loses interest, it means what they are doing is no longer holding their attention. It also means they do not want the job that they are supposed to do. I have seen some leaders busy themselves with everything else than their actual assignment. It is happening because they are bored. I believe leaders lose interest because they are being called to do something else. Many people who are called to build can experience this when they are called to develop and create something else. When we are real with ourselves and truthful with the Lord, we will know when it is time to do something else.

The lack of relevance is something that a seasoned leader should always consider and keep in mind. As generations progress, times change. If we are unwilling and unable to shift with the times, it may be time for us to consider making a shift into a different season. We know that our mission and message are always relevant, but the required methods of reaching the generations can change. We can't reach the world if we are still using 1950s and 1960s techniques. Sometimes the generations change so much that we are not in tune with the current issues. Many times, churches will see this when they notice a decline of young adults and youth in their churches; it can be a sign that there must be a change in leadership. The leader doesn't have to quit but readjust their efforts and attention. It can happen in business—when a company that has functioned a certain way for years, may see a decline in purchases and clients due to the declining demand for their business. When this happens, it is important to find ways to make sure that the company is maintaining relevance. The change may mean getting new voices and thinkers at the table to lead the organization. The seasoned leader's role may not be to lead the efforts of change but to counsel and guide.

As leaders age, their bodies cannot keep up with the pace of their assignment, and they begin to experience physical ailments and fatigue. Sometimes, fatigue does not have anything to do with age, but space in life and being overworked. When a person is experiencing consistent ailments that are hindering the organization's progress, they should consider readjusting their involvement in the organization. Vision and progress should not be hindered because of an individual. Sometimes the stress of the position can be leading to the ailments being experienced. I knew of a leader who was sick and had to take an extended leave of absence to heal and recover. They continued to have episodes of fatigue and sickness. Eventually, decided to leave their position and have not had another episode of sickness.

I want to emphasize that I am not saying that everyone who experiences ailments should retire. I am not saying that every older person should resign. I'm definitely not saying just because an organization is going through a low season that the leader is to be blamed, and they must quit. I am simply saying that leaders should consider what is going on and make decisions based on the organization's health. The primary key in all of this is being open to the Lord and His leading. God will lead and direct us if we are honest with Him and ourselves. As long as we have breath in our bodies, we have a task to do. In everything that we do, let's make sure that we are open to the direction of God. The legacy season is the time where God allows us to rest a little more, pour out, impart, and enjoy what we have been blessed to build. One should not have a hustle mindset when they should be in a place of reflection. This season is a gift to those who are faithful to God and have been used by Him to build something great on the earth. It is one that should be embraced and maximized. We maximize this season by pouring into as many people as we can and investing all our wisdom to make sure there is a continuity in the assignment that we have been called to steward on the earth. May your life's work continue for generations beyond your lifetime.

> **MAY YOUR LIFE'S WORK CONTINUE FOR GENERATIONS AND BEYOND YOUR LIFETIME.**

CHAPTER 8

Becoming a Transformational Leader

Everyone has been called to leadership! It is something that we have not heard enough in our society. Every Christian is a leader. When we receive Jesus as our Lord and savior, He calls each of us to carry out the great commission. It is in this reality that we find ourselves in the place of needing leadership cultivation and development. This calling is something that we must embrace and walk into to be effective in our life as believers. Because every Christian is a leader, every Christian should be developed in their leadership. Leadership development is an ongoing process, and it should essentially be a life mission. As leaders, we should always be pursuing greater knowledge so that we can be the most impactful in our assignments.

I started this book by speaking on the need for greater leadership in our society. I even went as far as to say that we are in a leadership deficit. As explained earlier, I believe this deficit is because there are many believers who are not occupying their position of leadership. There are certain movements that really press the idea of occupancy. These move-

AS LEADERS, WE SHOULD ALWAYS BE PURSUING.

ment's really train people to understand their call to lead in various other areas of society. An issue that we run into is that many people are not equipped with the tools necessary to be sustained as a leader.

Have you ever witnessed a person that has been given an opportunity to lead, but fail terribly? Or a person who has all the qualifications to be a great leader, but their character gets in the way and turn out to be destructive for the organization? Have you seen a leader who is an emotional wreck and leads from a place of fear and insecurity? All these are signs of a greater problem. Gifts are given without repentance, but character is cultivated. The character of a leader is developed through process and training. Honestly, the best leaders are healthy leaders.

Nowadays, there are various buzzwords that we often hear, sayings that speak to employee and leadership health, work-life balance, soul care, self-care, and boundaries. Mental health and emotional intelligence are a few words that people and companies use often. These words and phrases promote individual mental health and professional balance. The concept of work-life balance is contradictory from many of the leadership models that have been exemplified in our history. It is especially true here in America. Our nation has been built on the ideas of hard work, grit, producing, and drive. The "American Dream" is even associated with the idea if one works hard enough, they can obtain the life they desire. The connection to success is always associated with hard work. It is true that hard work does pay off and produces positive results. However, just working hard is not the only component to true long-lasting success. Organizations are increasingly pushing these ideas that promote physical, emotional, and mental health for their teams. This push has been developed to assist in performance and retention. The old models of productivity left people feeling burned out and overworked. People lose passion in their job because the work was enjoyable but genuinely laborious. It is also true for the church. There are so many leaders and pastors who quit their assignments because of being fatigued. As a leader who is called to be a change agent in the earth, you must make sure that this does not happen to you.

STYLES OF LEADERSHIP

There are various leadership styles we see in organizations. In 1939, a group of researchers led by Kurt Lewin identified different styles of leadership. There have been further studies since then that have identified more distinct types of leadership. Lewin's early studies has been influential in the development of three leadership styles that have provided the baseline for other theories. The three main styles are authoritarian, participative and delegative. I will discuss others as well, but these styles give us an understanding to the basic models of leadership.

The authoritarian is known as the autocratic leader who dictates policies and procedures and directs the work done by the group. This style of leadership does not look for any meaningful input from the people they are directing. The idea is that the team is to do what the leaders say and that is that. We see this model in more traditional organizations and churches where the leaders voice is the final say. Research has proven that this style of leadership hinders creativity. An authoritarian model can still be productive, but it can limit the organization from developing its full potential because of the lack of "buy-in" from teammates and subordinates. It can produce a micromanagement culture that can be burdensome for the team and tiresome for the leader. Authoritarian leadership can be stifling but is best applied when there is little time for input from the group.

The participative style of leadership, also known as the democratic style, allows group members to feel connected to the decision-making process. These leaders participate with the team by offering guidance and input to the collective group while still maintaining the final say. Participative leadership causes their subordinates to feel like the leaders are a part of a team. This style can lead to a sense of ambiguity within the team. If participants are not mature, they can lose site of the leaders' role to lead. It can bring about miscommunication, mistrust amongst the team and confusion. A leader that uses this model must practice strong boundaries and be self-aware in their approach with the team.

The delegative leadership practices is a very hands-off approach. This type of leader offers little to no guidance to the team and leaves the decision making to the group. The leader will provide the resources to be successful and then hand over the power to the group to be successful. The delegative style doesn't offer much guidance and is proven to be the least productive. It works the best when a team is full of highly competent workers who prefer less directorial input. This style works best with creatives and is challenging with a group that lacks the needed skills and needs more development.

Other models that have been discovered over time are transactional leadership, charismatic leadership, transformational leadership, and servant leadership. The model that I have found to be the most effective is the transformational leadership model. It was first described during the late 1970's, by researcher Bernard M. Bass. He has been noted for expanding the concept of transformation leadership further. Transformational leaders can motivate and inspire their followers, this in turn leads to positive changes in the group. Authentic transformational leaders are emotionally intelligent, energetic, and passionate. These leaders focus on making sure their team reaches their full potential, this then causes the organization to achieve its goals. Studies have shown that this style of leadership results in higher performance. This style places the focus on the followers. A transformational leader is concerned about the people they are leading.

Here are the components of a transformational leader:
- Transformational leadership requires intellectual stimulation, individualized consideration, inspirational motivation, and idealized influence. Intellectual stimulation speaks of a person who can challenge what is considered normal and encourage people to be creative.

- Transformational leaders can encourage people to diversify processes and engage in new learning opportunities.

- True transformational leaders and thinkers can be individually considerate. This happens by offering support to individuals. They place a greater value on people as individuals than as a conglomerate. Followers feel the freedom to share their ideas and receive direct recognition for their contributions. The third component is inspirational motivation.

- Transformational leaders can articulate their vision clearly. They can inspire people to receive the same passion in accomplishing the goals expressed by the leader. The last component is idealized influence. This transformational leader can be a role model to the team that they are leading. The followers trust and respect the leader and they desire to be like their leader. This type of leader has earned the respect of the team and they want to support the vision because they believe that the leader is worth following.

As stated earlier, I believe that the best leadership style is the transformational model. This leadership approach truly focuses on the personal development and health of the leader. When the leader does their work and then leads from a healthy place, they can create a healthy organization and team. Often, people blame the demise of a movement on the people without taking an introspective look at their contribution to the problem. A transformational leader is constantly developing themselves to make sure that they can assist in the development of others. The work of a transformational leader starts within. You cannot lead people in this manner if you have not done the work of internal transformation.

Every Christian leader should be a transformational thinker and leader. As Christians, we are called to be transformed.

Romans 12:1-2 says,

"I beseech you therefore, brethren, by the mercies of God, that ye present your bodies a living sacrifice, holy, acceptable unto God, which is your reasonable service. And be not conformed to this world: but be ye transformed by the renewing of your mind, that ye may prove what is that good, and acceptable, and perfect, will of God."

The word "conformed" here means to be similar. This speaks of possessing the inner essence, identity, or showing similar behavior from having the same nature. The scripture is telling us not to possess the same inner essence as the world. We are not to be identified with the ways of the world. When the Bible speaks of "this world" it is speaking of the age or the way of life. We know that Satan is the prince of this world and that he works to influence public thought and opinion. We are not to have the same essence as the people who are being influenced by Satan. We are called to be "transformed." This word speaks of a metamorphosis. We are called to have an inward change that makes us completely different from the world. Metamorphosis gives us the imagery of a caterpillar being turned into a butterfly. We are to be completely different from the world. This transformation happens when we submit to God and his will. This is not a religious outward transformation but a transformation of mind, heart, and spirit. This is a person who has been changed through the power of God and they live a life that is totally different from the world around them. Transformational leadership happens first within the leader and then the leader is essential in assisting other people experiencing transformation. The idea of renewing one's mind happens by a day-by-day process of walking with the Lord.

The only way for a leader to be truly transformational is to be spiritually renewed and regenerated. When we are renewed, we can lead from the inside out. So many times, we focus on the company or the team, but honestly, they are a byproduct of the leadership. We must exemplify health in all the components of our life. We must be healthy in our body, mind, and spirit. I have witnessed people focus on the task at hand, and not on how they are doing personally; God wants us to be healthy personally, and spiritually so our leadership is effective. The way that we truly make sure we are healthy internally is by focusing on our spiritual formation.

Spiritual formation focuses on the deepening of one's relationship with God.

2 Corinthians 3:17-18 says,
"Now the Lord is the Spirit; and where the Spirit of the Lord is, there is liberty. But we all, with unveiled face, beholding as in a mirror the glory of the Lord, are being transformed into the same image from glory to glory, just as by the Spirit of the Lord."

We are spiritually formed by spending time with the Lord. I am privileged to be born to a family of believers who are praying people. Every day, I watched my mother and grandmother spend time with the Lord. Every morning, I would see my mother sit in her prayer chair in the living room and pray for our family. Naturally after seeing this all my life growing up, I started the same practice. I was never taught what a spiritual discipline was, all I knew is that I should wake up and read my Bible daily. This practice has been my saving grace all my life. Consistent spiritual practices are the key to making sure a leader is transformational. We see in scripture that Jesus would often withdraw away from the crowds to pray and spend time with the Father. I am confident that it was Jesus' prayer life that helped him to stay on course regarding His earthly assignment.

I learned prayer and Bible reading from my mother and grandmother, but through my own time I have come to learn that there are more disciplines than these two. Spiritual disciplines are categorized in three different ways—internal disciplines, external disciplines, and corporate disciplines. Internal disciplines are meditation, prayer, fasting, and study. These disciplines assist the individual in building up their spirit. Leaders should make internal disciplines apart of their everyday schedule. External disciplines are simplicity, solitude, submission, and service. These disciplines are attitudes that we should aim to possess and things that we should seek to practice often. Corporate disciplines are completed within the context of the greater body of the church. These include, confession, worship, giving, and celebration. Author Richard Foster, in his book, *Celebration Of Discipline*, has great resources that can assist in learning more about these disciplines.

God wants you to be whole. Wholeness is the true calling for leadership. We are living in a day where we are seeing so many talented leaders fall. The failure that we are witnessing is typically due to character, integrity, and brokenness. God allows us time to be processed so that we don't have to walk in the traps of the enemy. Allowing yourself to be developed from the inside out and placing a priority on your spiritual well-being is essential to maintain great character as you lead. The process of development should never be rushed nor avoided. Everything that we experience is intended to shape us into becoming more like Christ. Leaders who rush through the processes of development and make poor investments into their spiritual deposit are never able to end well. A transformational leader is focused on making sure they can lead from a life that has been poured into by the Father.

GOD WANTS YOU TO BE WHOLE.

Moses had many issues. He was an excellent leader. Moses did not always make the best decisions, but his time with God definitely fueled his leadership. I respect that he was not only the leader of the nation, but he was the intercessor for the nation. His revelation and direction were all granted to him by his time spent with God. When we dedicate our life to God and give Him access to shape us, we are then able to lead effectively. God wants leaders to be renewed spiritually and raised as leaders who are committed to spending time with God. God wants leaders who are intercessors. Leaders should be people who are connected to the source and are praying for the advancement of what they are leading.

In whatever season you are in, God wants to make sure He has your heart. I will go so far as to say that our devotional life is the greatest asset that we can possess as Christian leaders. Our time with the Lord gives us the ability to deal with issues of the world. Please remember that the assignment that you have is a ministry and with that, you will be attacked. The way to stay grounded in all that you do is making sure that you are allowing God to consistently build you up. We are built by times spent with God. Never forsake this time and never put it on the back burner; always make sure that your life with God is the central aspect of your life.

> **IN WHATEVER SEASON YOU ARE IN, GOD WANTS TO MAKE SURE HE HAS YOUR HEART.**

Transformational leadership speaks of a leader who has been transformed and who is consistently being transformed. This process is one of growth. Every season is an opportunity to learn and to grow. The Lord is calling for us to grow and reflect Him on the earth. In Luke 19, we see the parable of the businessman that leaves his servant with various talents (money). In the parable, he gives different amounts of money to each servant and tells them that he was going on a long journey and that they should "occupy" until he returned. This parable is typically taught as a lesson on stewardship. It is common to use this scripture to teach people to make sure they invest their gifts well so they can give the Lord a good return on his investment in their life.

> **TRANSOFRMATIONAL LEADERSHIP SPEAKS OF A LEADER WHO HAS BEEN TRANSFORMED AND WHO IS CONSISTENTLY BEING TRANSFORMED.**

As a pastor, I love using this parable as a lesson of stewardship. Parables are amazing! I love how the Lord Jesus, the master teacher, used parables reflecting real life concepts of the day to explain spiritual truths. Parables are earthly stories to reveal the concepts of the kingdom of God. I believe this teaching is layered. Yes, I believe it speaks of stewardship, but I also believe there is another idea that the Lord is trying to give us. I believe this parable gives us an understanding of our assignment on the earth as we await the Lord's return. Jesus tells His disciples in John 14:3, "I go to prepare a place for you." In the same way that this ruler was leaving for a journey, I believe Jesus was describing how He would leave the disciples on the earth. The Master left resources for His servants and told them to occupy. This Master was telling His servants to continue His business until he returned to them. The Master gave them everything they needed (gifts, talents, resources) to continue the business until He returned. This parable presents an idea that when Jesus would leave to prepare a place for us that we would have to continue His business on the earth. This is essentially the great commission and the role of the church. We have been commissioned to continue the "business" or "work" of Christ on the earth. The work of Christ is His ministry. We have been called to continue the ministry of Christ until He returns. It is in this truth that we have the assignment to occupy.

Our leadership call is to carry the ministry of Christ to all the world. God is granting His people access to areas of society to lead and represent Him in those spaces. When you are granted a seat at the table, they do not need a leader who leads from a carnal or earthly framework. They need a leader who is transformed and renewed; a leader who reflects the image of God. A transformational leader is dedicated to doing the consistent work of being changed into the image of Jesus.

> *"But we all, with unveiled face, beholding as in a mirror the glory of the Lord, are being transformed into the same image from glory to glory, just as by the Spirit of the Lord."*
>
> 2 Corinthians 3:18

CHAPTER 9

Understanding the Call and the Assignment

One story in scripture that I find so interesting is the story of the young Jesus who gets lost in the caravan home from Jerusalem. I imagine Mary and Joseph being nervous wrecks when they realized that they lost their son in the crowd of people. For some reason I picture the scene from *Home Alone* when Kevin's mom realizes that he was not with the family. I can see Mary screaming hysterically when she realizes that Jesus is nowhere to be found amongst the crowd. I can hear Mary screaming JESUS!!! JESUS!!! JESUS!!!!! In their hysteria they turn around from their journey to go back to Jerusalem to try to find their son. I have two princesses, Gabrielle and Grace, and I absolutely love and adore them. I know that my little ladies are God sent and I love them with all my heart. The idea of losing them in a crowd of people is a horrifying thought. It is safe to say that Mary and Joseph felt this way about their son. However in addition to him being their son, there is the whole part about him being the Messiah. Both parents were aware that they had been privileged to raise the Savior of the world. Can you imagine the devastation this detail adds to the story? They lost their son, but they lost the Savior of the world. (I just wrote that and felt anxious). As the story continues, they turn around from their journey and frantically look for Jesus. They eventually find Him in the temple sitting and conversing with the rabbis in the temple. Mary says to Jesus,

So when they saw Him, they were amazed; and His mother said to Him, "Son, why have You done this to us? Look, Your father and I have sought You anxiously."

Luke 2:48

Jesus response is so intriguing to me. Jesus responds to His mother asking why she would be looking for Him, didn't they know that He would be about His Father's business? Jesus is wondering why they were so alarmed, He wasn't the kind of kid to wonder, if He would be doing anything, it would be something eternally purposeful. Jesus was sure of His assignment at the age of 12. This is one of many facts about Jesus as a person that inspires me. Jesus knew His assignment and was focused on accomplishing it.

John 20 gives tells the story of the disciples after the resurrection. The Bible tells us that the disciples were hiding in a locked room because of their fear. They had recently witnessed their Savior brutally killed and they were afraid that they were next. Jesus appears to them (please understand that the room was locked and Jesus walked through the walls). When He appeared to them they were afraid because they thought that it was a ghost. Jesus spoke peace to them and showed His scars. This passage of scripture is actually John's version of the great commission.

In John 20:21 Jesus says,
So Jesus said to them again, "Peace to you! As the Father has sent Me, I also send you."

Jesus was a man on assignment. In Genesis 3, God gives the first Messianic prophecy about Jesus. He tells Eve that her seed would destroy the head of the serpent. All throughout the Old Testament, people received prophetic insight and declared the coming of the Messiah. When Christ comes on the scene, He is the manifestation of prophetic words that were spoken thousands of years before His birth. He is sent to the world for one mission.

John 3:16 says,
"For God so loved that world that he gave his only begotten son that whosoever believed Him should not perish but have everlasting life."

Jesus came to the earth to save people from their sins and to reconnect them to the eternal love of the Father. Jesus came to the earth on a mission. The word "send" in John 20:21 comes from the word "Apostolos." This word is a governmental word and it speaks of a delegate or a messenger that is sent on an assignment. A person that is "sent" is a person that has orders from a superior to carry a message or to complete a task. Jesus is telling His disciples that the same way He was sent from Heaven to the earth for a particular assignment, they are to do the same thing. All followers of Christ have been called to carry an assignment that is ordered by Heaven. We have been called to be its delegates in the earth. A major premise of this book is to connect this heavenly assignment to the call of leadership. It is in your delegated delegated assignment that you will find your delegated call to leadership.

Observing the life of Jesus is a brilliant case study for leadership. I believe it is this sense of calling and assignment that kept Him through the rough parts of His earthly life. Jesus endured so much but He was willing to do it because He knew that He was on the earth as a delegate of Heaven. He had a mission in mind. We see this truth when He was in the garden sweeting blood agonizing over the fact that He was going to have to die on the cross. He prayed and asked the Lord if there was another way. He wanted the responsibility to be taken from Him. In His time of prayer, He reconciled with the idea that what He had to go through was the will of God. He submitted to the cross because the assignment that He carried was greater than the pain that He would endure. He endured the cross because He knew that mankind needed salvation. Having a sense of purpose can be a keeping measure for people to stay focused.

Hebrews 12:2 says
"looking unto Jesus, the author and finisher of our faith, who for the joy that was set before Him endured the cross, despising the shame, and has sat down at the right hand of the throne of God."

The author of Hebrews says that Jesus endured the cross because of the joy that was set before Him. His perspective was kept in line because of His sense of call.

The only way to be a successful leader who finishes well and completes the assignment is to have a strong sense of calling and conviction. As a leader, you must be clear of the call and focused on the call. In Chapter 3, I discussed the season of invitation and how this season is the time where people are "called" into their assignment. In this chapter, I want to build on that concept and provide greater depth to help to open your mind regarding this aspect of leadership. All believers are invited to serve the Lord and to complete their assignment in the earth. In essence, this calling is a prophetic call. Now please don't run off and tell anyone that I have called you a prophet! And please don't use this concept as a justification for your self-proclaimed "prophetic assignment." However, strive to seek to understand this idea in the truest manner that is written. Your calling into leadership is prophetic because of the fact that it is expressed from the mind of God and has a connection to an eternal purpose.

Let's define the word "prophetic." The word prophetic describes something that will happen in the future. Some synonyms of this word are predict, foretell, foresee and forecast. Prophecy is a word that speaks of the foretelling of something that will come. Prophecy is also forthtelling. This means that prophecy is speaking the truth and expressing the mind of God in regards to the affairs of man. Being prophetic is two-fold, being a prophetic person is one who will speak truth to power and secondly speaking a direct word from the Lord. We know that Jesus was the manifestation of prophecy. Prophets spoke of His coming and He was the fulfillment of things spoken before His birth. Biblically we see prophets ministering in both context. We see Isaiah prophesying God's heart regarding Israel, and we see Elijah confronting Ahab and Jezebel.

Revelation 19:10 says,
"For the testimony of Jesus is the spirit of prophecy."

This scripture tells us that true prophecy bears the message of Jesus. All prophecies should point to Christ. Any word that is given that is not connected to the message of Jesus or His eternal purpose is a false prophecy. When God calls a leader it is a call to reveal the heart of God for a particular area of society. The assignment is a manifestation of a prophetic need in the earth.

Essentially, you would not be called to do it if the Lord did not plan for it. God's call on your life is a prophetic call to foretell or forthtell the truth of Jesus to that particular field of influence. The burden that you have to start a business is not from your own mind, it is a call of God to address a need in the earth. Your desire to pursue that career path is not from your own mind, but it is a call of God to impact that arena. Your call as a leader is a prophetic assignment.

Prophetic leadership understands that the need for their presence in a role of influence is connected to a greater assignment. Christians are sent into areas as ambassadors of Heaven to communicate the heart of God. Moses is an example of this. His life assignment was a response to a prophetic call. He was a prophetic leader because he was sent to the children of Israel as a response to their cries and bondage. Moses had the responsibility of communicating to Pharoah (representing an oppressive system) the word of the Lord. You must recognize that your leadership is not just for your resumé. Your leadership comes with a responsibility to share the heart of God. Your leadership means that you are responsible for promoting the plans of God in the place that you are called for. As you move forward in your area of influence you must keep in mind that you are a representative of Heaven. You have the mandate to proclaim the truth even when it is unpopular. The spirit of this day and age is always attempting to silence the voice of the Lord.

This spirit desires to intimidate believers, especially Christian leaders, to not speak against the injustice and wickedness of society. Prophetic leadership accepts the call to be light in darkness and seeks for every opportunity to shine the light of God. My wife is called into education. She was commissioned by God through a prophetic vision regarding her assignment to build schools. Her desire was to be a news anchor, but the Lord put the burden of education on her in college. Our callings are different. I know that I have been called a priest. I am a minister of the gospel and I have been called to serve the body as a vocational minister. My wife, on the other hand, is a minister of the gospel, but one way that her ministry is expressed is through her career as an educator. I have had a front row view of God's consistent development of calling and purpose in her life. I have watched her teach in the roughest communities with children who have experienced severe trauma. I have seen her minister and advocate for children who were deemed to be troublemakers. She has had to speak up against teachers and school leaders who sought to label children and set them on a course of destruction because they were culturally unaware of how to deal with the students' needs. As a school leader and administrator, she had to lead conversations and trainings to empower teachers to be more culturally responsive in their approaches to inner city kids. As a consultant, I have seen God use her to challenge schools to understand and respond appropriately to various challenges associated with diversity. I have countless stories of my wife serving her field as a prophetic voice.

One of my favorite stories of her classroom days is the time that she told a child to tell their anger to go and that it was not welcome in their body or in her classroom. She essentially led the child through a deliverance exercise. As a prophetically called educator, she has had the responsibility to show up in her sphere and represent God to secular institutions. Please hear me! This type of leadership is never effective when we push our Christian views through religious banter and judgmental attitudes. This type of leadership is the most impactful when a Christian shows up and is present to serve in the best way possible. This service is not a loud declaration that is spoken, but it is a life declaration that is experienced from those we serve and work alongside. Prophetic leaders understand that gospel is the most profound when it is experienced. No one has to know that we have been "called" to do what we do. All they need to know is that there is something different about how we do what we do.

I am always amazed when I meet people who believe that Christians have to only serve in ministry in a Christian context. There are people who think that a Christian teacher has to teach in a Christian school, or a Christian singer has to be a Christian singer, or a Christian actor can only act in movies targeted for Christians. The divide between things considered sacred and things secular has had polarizing impact. There is no way that a call from God could be secular, even if it is not expressed in a Christian context. We are living in a day where we need people who are intentional about serving in secular arenas. The key is making sure that we show up and are faithful to our God, faith, and convictions while leading in spaces that are secular. God is calling for leaders to serve with faithful presence. Jesus is the best example for this. Jesus' earthly ministry was for the lost people of Israel. He did not focus His teaching to impact the religious leaders of His day. In fact, those leaders opposed Him and were the ones who found grounds for His crucifixion. It was the religious people of His day that killed him. Jesus was the Son of God, but His assignment was experienced by those who were the most broken. Jesus was amongst the common people. Jesus ministered to the crooks of His day. Jesus walked with people who were considered sinners.

One of the names of Christ is the name "Emanuel." This name means "God with us." Jesus was God incarnated in the earth. Although Jesus was fully man, He was God living amongst mankind as a man. I know this concept can be hard to understand, but it is this truth that we see the very power of the Gospel. God sent Jesus to save us from our sins. When God created the heavens and the earth, He assigned mankind to be the ruler of the world. He called mankind to be the gatekeepers of the earth. When Adam and Eve sinned, they allowed the power of the enemy to be released in the earth. Since Adam, a man, sinned, we need a man to fix the problem. God will never go against the order of His creation. Jesus had to come to earth as a man to save us from the hand of the enemy. We could not have been saved unless Jesus was amongst us as a man. He had to die on the cross as a man to bring us back to God. We needed God's incarnational presence.

All throughout scripture we see God using men to bring His plan of salvation for mankind. Moses' assignment to lead the people of Israel out of their bondage in Egypt to their promised land was a response to years of cries and prayers for deliverance. Moses was sent as an answered prayer. Moses embodied the love of God for the people of Israel. David was burdened to kill Goliath after hearing how he insulted God's people. His passion was not his pride, but a righteous call to deliver God's people from their oppression. Esther's position as queen was an assignment of God to prevent the destruction of God's people. If she would have not been in the palace, she would not have had the favor of the king. Elijah's ministry came from a place of a need. The people of Israel were living in a spiritual vacuum and the Lord raised up a prophet that would be bold enough to stand against Jezebel and Ahab's wickedness. Elijah was sent as a vessel of God. There are more examples than these. However these examples reveal God's way of dealing with human problems. He responds by raising up a

human being to represent Him. It is what we call incarnational presence.

God saved the world by sending Jesus who was God in flesh. The way that He desires to continually change the world is by sending those who He has called to represent Him. When a leader understands their prophetic call, they are then called to serve incarnationally. This means that they lead and serve knowing that they are called to represent Jesus. God is calling for leaders to emerge and be incarnational in their communities, businesses, in their careers, and in every aspect of life. It is true that we are sometimes the only Bible that people read. How we live our life can impact what people see and understand of Jesus.

Incarnational leadership seeks to take the shared experiences and plights of those whom they serve and lead to implement improvements for others. In order to be incarnational, one must know the experiences of those they are leading. They must have an understanding. The Bible speaks of Jesus' knowledge of the human experience and his ability to empathize our struggles.

> In Hebrews 4:15, it says,
> *"For we do not have a High Priest who cannot sympathize with our weaknesses, but was in all points tempted as we are, yet without sin."*

It is because of Jesus' incarnational ministry that He is currently able to intercede for us. He can minister to us because He understands. Many leaders function above the team. Many leaders have no clue of what the team is experiencing. To truly serve people well, we must be close to the people and understand the experience. The process of becoming incarnational is all about humility.

Leaders must humbly submit to the instruction, experience and knowledge of the people they are serving. An example of this is a teacher from the suburbs moving to the inner city to live in the same area as their students. Becoming incarnational requires a heart to learn and be one with a team. Your calling is prophetic, and a prophetic call requires us to have true experienced knowledge. As an incarnational leader, it is imperative to take off all accolades celebrated by society and connect on a human level. This attitude moves from compassion, to empathy, to passion, to advocacy, to justice. All leaders are called to be a solution to a problem. The only way to fix the problem is to understand the problem.

There are various ways to become incarnational. I know many people who have moved to become one with communities to be able to serve them well. Some pastors make it a point to live in the area that their church is located. I have been privileged to work with a large mission serving on Skid Row in Los Angeles for over four years. My friend and mentor, Albert, is a program director for this mission serving single men who are experiencing homelessness. He is a brilliant theologian, excellent counselor, pastor and overall great guy. Albert has had experience with addiction personally. However, his personal life experiences didn't warrant him an expert on things related to drugs, the prison system, the crises in Los Angeles surrounding homelessness and life on Skid Row. Again, this man is brilliant, but his formal education did not prepare him to be effective in reaching this particular demographic. He shared with me how he would go to the common areas where the men would hang out. With no agenda, he would go to the smoking areas, the lunchroom, day rooms and other places to just be around the men that he was serving.

It led him to develop a rapport with the men. He also gained respect but most importantly, he gained an understanding of the climate of his ministry. His time around the men taught him how to best serve them. He saw the men when their defenses were down and when they were in a comfortable environment. He learned how to reach them authentically. Incarnational ministry is more about seeking to understand, than trying to make people understand. Making people understand is one of the biggest issues that I have seen in my years of participating with compassion ministries. In the Western world, we assume that our success, education, and life experiences make us superior. It is almost like we have a superiority complex. It is in this where we get our savior complexes and hero syndromes. We go on mission trips with the idea that our two-week visit is going to change a national crisis that has existed for centuries. Or our one-time food donations around Thanksgiving are going to change the homeless crisis. We go to serve with the idea that we have so much to give. This mindset weakens the model for ministry because it divides as opposed to uniting. Incarnational ministry intentionally says I do not know, but I am seeking to understand. As we understand we are able to make the changes necessary to benefit those that our assignment serves.

An incarnational approach values relationships and people. It is the mindset of "teach me life" from your vantage point and not "learn life" from my vantage point. This mindset teaches me about you so that we can walk together in unity. As a leader, when you understand the needs of the team and the people that your industry is serving you can properly empower. As an incarnational leader, you learn to empower from the relationship that is built. In discovery and humility, you will see the gifts of the people that you are serving. You will also understand that what is typically needed to change or impact the team is actually in the team. You will learn that the gifts and skills to change a community are in the community. Your role as a prophetically inspired incarnational leader is to strengthen, guide, and serve. As a leader, we are servants of God called to serve humanity by representing His heart for them. We are called to let people know that He loves them and that He has a plan to restore them. You may read this and say to yourself, this sounds so "ministry" focused. How does this apply to me since I am a businessperson? How does this apply to me when I am in the medical field?

Here is the thing, all industries are intended to benefit human life in some way. The way to be impactful in whatever industry you are in is to understand the people, places, and things you are serving. When you can speak to the experience because of your experience, you can maximize your impact. God is calling for us to represent Him. Our calling to represent God should be by any means necessary. Our assignment is to impact the world! We are called to leave the world better than how we received it. In every generation, we are given the opportunity to build off what has happened in the past. We are blessed with history to learn from the victories and failures of people who have gone before us. As a leader, you can build something that makes history. Remember that you are called by God, your assignment is prophetic. God wants you to address the areas in the world that are in great need. He prophetically called you to be an incarnational leader.

Epilogue

I am passionate about leadership. I am also passionate in my call to raise up leaders to understand their calling and assignment. I feel that God has assigned me to encourage my generation to be as stellar as possible. I also feel called to help believers see how they are uniquely wired to answer the issues of the day. I am certain that we are born intentionally to serve in the time where our gift is the most needed. We would not be here on this planet if there wasn't something special that we can contribute to. It is my prayer that you have felt inspired as you have read this book. I also pray that you have felt challenged to seek to understand your season and then to maximize it. I want you to serve God and be wonderful in all that you have been called to do.

You are a leader! You have a place where you have been called to lead. You are extraordinary! God is seeking to grow you in incredible ways. Because you are a child of God and He has called you, your potential is limitless. Do not limit yourself. The only limitation we have is the one we put on ourselves. The world would try to put you in various boxes because of how the systems of man are made. We are finite and we live in a finite reality. Our reality has multiple limitations. Here is the beauty about being called by God, we are called from the perspective of Heaven. God places eternal plans in mortal people. Your assignment has been decreed from Heaven. It means there is no cap on how much you can grow and be developed to be effective in your assignment. The only limitation we have is that we are in a world where time matters. Time is precious and it should be valued. It is precious because it can work against us. When we waste time, those are years off of our lives that we never get back. You have been born in time to impact the world during your lifetime. We do not have time to waste. Whatever season you are in, make it a point to do well in that season. Be about your Father's business. You have read this book because it is your time to EMERGE! This is the time for you to walk in what God has called you to do. This is your time. Don't waste it! God has placed you here because the earth is waiting for you to come forth.

Acknowledgments

Thank you to my mother, Michaellyn Rush; thank you for being incredible. You are a rock and have been the wind beneath my wings my entire life. Thank you for praying for me so consistently.

Thank you, Willa Robinson and the KP Publishing Team. You have been a delight to work with and thank you for walking me through to the finish line. I am grateful to you.

Thank you to all the pastors and senior leaders who have mentored me over the years.

About the Author

Dr. Robert Randolph Rush, III,

Commissioned by God to "Build My People," Dr. Robert Randolph Rush III is passionate about edifying and encouraging individuals to live optimally. Robert has dedicated his life to serve as an encouragement to the Body of Christ. Having been characterized as a revolutionary leader within the emerging generation, Robert exemplifies the spirit of wisdom and possesses an undeniable anointing for teaching and preaching. He is an effective strategist and travels to train and mobilize emerging leaders for national transformation. Robert has ministered both nationally and internationally, sharing biblical truths that have brought many lives to the knowledge of God. He feels compelled to motivate individuals to think from a higher perspective. Robert is the founder of R.U.S.H. Ministries, a teaching ministry that is dedicated to serve as an educational resource to churches and ministries. He and his wife are the founders and pastors of Impact Church Los Angeles. Robert holds a bachelor's degree in Business Marketing, a master's degree in Practical Theology and a Doctorate in Transformational Leadership. He is honored to do life and ministry with the love of his life, Brittany Rush. They have two daughters, Gabrielle Taylor and Grace Alexandria Rush, and reside in Southern California.